ACADEMIC COMPETITIONS
for Gifted Students

A Resource Book for Teachers and Parents

Mary K. Tallent-Runnels
Ann C. Candler-Lotven

CORWIN PRESS
A SAGE Company
Thousand Oaks, CA 91320

For information:

Corwin Press
A SAGE Company
2455 Teller Road
Thousand Oaks, California 91320
www.corwinpress.com

SAGE India Pvt. Ltd.
B 1/I 1 Mohan Cooperative
   Industrial Area
Mathura Road, New Delhi 110 044
India

SAGE Ltd.
1 Oliver's Yard
55 City Road
London EC1Y 1SP
United Kingdom

SAGE Asia-Pacific Pte. Ltd.
33 Pekin Street #02-01
Far East Square
Singapore 048763

Printed in the United States of America.

Library of Congress Cataloging-in-Publication Data

Tallent-Runnels, Mary K.
Academic competitions for gifted students : a resource book for teachers and parents / by Mary K. Tallent-Runnels and Ann C. Candler-Lotven. — 2nd ed.
    p. cm.
Includes bibliographical references and index.
ISBN 978-1-4129-5910-0 (cloth)
ISBN 978-1-4129-5911-7 (pbk.)
    1. School contests—United States. 2. Gifted children—Education—United States. I. Candler-Lotven, Ann C. II. Title.

LB3068.T35 2008
371.95—dc22

This book is printed on acid-free paper.

07 08 09 10 11   10 9 8 7 6 5 4 3 2 1

Acquisitions Editor:	Allyson P. Sharp
Managing Editor:	David Chao
Editorial Assistant:	Mary Dang
Production Editor:	Cassandra Margaret Seibel
Copy Editor:	Kathy Anne Savadel
Typesetter:	C&M Digitals (P) Ltd.
Proofreader:	Kris Bergstad
Indexer:	Jean Casalegno
Cover Designer:	Karine Hovsepian

Contents

Preface

We believe that this book will be valuable for everyone who works with or lives with children from kindergarten through Grade 12. It resulted from our need to help others find out about available competitions and to realize the joy of competing. Joining in the work of competition can challenge children to go beyond the regular school curriculum to achieve their goals.

Children can benefit from participation in academic competitions. However, many people know little or nothing about the many competitions suitable for gifted and other talented students that are offered throughout the United States. This book serves as a quick, efficient way to locate and evaluate them.

The number of competitions continues to grow each year. With decreased funding for schools, these programs become viable, less expensive alternatives, supplements, or options in school programs. With a finite amount of money to spend in the schools, teachers need to make more informed choices about which competitions they might choose for their students. With the advent of site-based management, teachers are the ones who decide where much of the money will go.

This book offers criteria for selecting and implementing competitions in light of students' strengths and weaknesses. It will be a handy reference to help you find out about competitions in several content areas for students from kindergarten through the twelfth grade. After consulting several books that list names of competitions, we decided that what was needed was a book that would not only focus on academic competitions but also offer information to help teachers guide students through competitions and avoid the possible negative effects of competing.

Therefore, the purpose of this book is to help teachers, gifted program coordinators, other administrators, and parents find out about many academic competitions and to give them tips on how to use competitions in a beneficial manner with children. Readers of this book will find out about contact people and how to participate in each of the contests. In short, this book will enable parents and teachers to access these programs easily. Teachers and gifted program coordinators will be able to use our book as a quick, efficient way to locate information about competitions. We believe that our book will also be valuable to professors who teach courses in gifted education and want to learn about competitions; it will also help teachers learn about outlets allowing children to compete in an area of interest.

In this second edition, we list more than twice as many competitions as in the first edition. We also updated the research on competitions and on characteristics of students. The list of local organizations we provided in the first edition no longer offered assistance in finding other contests. Therefore, we deleted that section in this second edition and instead provide some Web sites that update their lists of competitions. We also added a section in the indexes that identifies which of the competitions can be entered from home or from home schools. Finally, we added a new index to this second edition that lists competitions that are directed especially toward special populations. This includes contests for members of ethnic–minority groups as well as contests for students with special needs.

The first chapter of this book is intended to provide an introduction and overview of characteristics of good competitions or ways to evaluate them. It also discusses competition and its impact on talented students. Adults who guide students through competitions must understand the way participation can affect these students. Specifically, we ask the reader to consider the role of competition in light of the characteristics and needs of the particular students with whom he or she is working. Ways to anticipate and avoid potential problems with competition are identified and discussed, as are strategies for maximizing the benefits of competitions. We want teachers and parents to help children believe that winning is not the sole goal of competition. The second chapter includes a description of each of the international and national competitions we have identified. The collection of contests is not intended to be exhaustive, and we hope readers will let us know of more. The "Web Sites for Finding Other Competitions" index provides information on finding local and state programs not included in our book. This empowers readers to learn more. Strategies for locating other sources of competitions are presented, along with directories and Web sites to assist in contacting appropriate information sources. Finally, the book includes two indexes designed to aid in locating the competitions. The indexes group the competitions by title, subject area, and grade level.

Mary K. Tallent-Runnels
Ann C. Candler-Lotven

Acknowledgments

W e are grateful to Mary's graduate assistant, Katie M. Rhode, for helping us with research and with making sense of all the information out there. She spent countless hours contributing to this work. Thanks also to *G/C/T* magazine for all the helpful competitions listed there. *G/C/T* is a great resource.

Corwin Press gratefully thanks the following reviewers for their contributions to this book:

Kay L. Gibson
Professor, Curriculum & Instruction
Wichita State University, KS

Jessica Ann Hockett
Graduate student/teacher
University of Virginia
Charlottesville, VA

Barbara Polnick
Assistant Professor, Educational Leadership and Counseling
Sam Houston State University
Huntsville, TX

Susan Shachar
Coordinator of Programs for Academic & Creative Enrichment
Stephen S. Wise Temple Elementary School
Woodland Hills, CA

Joan Smutny
Author, gifted specialist
National-Louis University
Wilmette, IL

About the Authors

 **Mary K. Tallent-Runnels** is Professor of Educational Psychology in the College of Education at Texas Tech University. She has over thirty years of experience working with parents and teachers of gifted children ages four through seventeen. In addition to her time as both a public and private school teacher of gifted students and administrator of gifted programs, she is the former director of the IDEAL program at Texas Tech University. She is the recipient of several teaching and research awards at both the public school and university levels. Her research interests are gifted children and online instruction. She is the author of numerous articles in gifted and talented education as well as in online teaching. She has published in journals such as *Gifted Child Quarterly, Journal for the Education of the Gifted, Roeper Review, G/C/T, Contemporary Educational Psychology, Review of Educational Research*, and the *Journal of Experimental Education*.

 **Ann C. Candler-Lotven** is Provost and Vice President for Academic Affairs at Texas A&M University Texarkana. She has thirty years of experience in the education of students with exceptional characteristics. During those years, she also worked with the parents and teachers of exceptional students. Her research interests include exceptional learners, learning and student strategies, and gifted students. She has authored numerous articles, books, and book chapters in the field of special education. She has published in *Academic Therapy, Child Language Teaching and Therapy, Gifted Child Quarterly*, and the *Journal for the Education of the Gifted*.

Introduction

Making Decisions About Competitive Programs for Gifted Students

When we began writing the second edition of this book, we already knew that there were many wonderful contests and competitions. We narrowed our search to national and international competitions that we felt were suitable for bright, able youngsters. We then decided to exclude contests in athletics, dance, and music. We know that competition in those areas is important, but we decided to limit our book to academic competitions, as we did in our first edition.

We changed the content area of Computers to Technology, including robotics and related competitions. We also removed the area of drama and included only drama-related contests, such as playwriting. These were subsumed under Language Arts. The final list of content areas we chose included Technology, Foreign Language, General Problem Solving, Language Arts, Mathematics, Science, Social Studies, and Speech. We scoured newspapers and magazines for mention of contest winners. We asked our friends for their ideas, and then we asked their friends. We called organizers of contests we already knew about. Then we began to follow suggestions given to us on ways to search for more information.

As we continued to prepare for the second edition of this book, we realized times had changed since the first edition was published. We could now look on the Internet for so much more information. We were amazed at all the new opportunities available to gifted students and to other students capable of competing in these programs. We deleted all the competitions that were no longer active. We had seventy-nine academic competitions listed in our first edition, and we now have more than twice that many in this second edition. We are certainly aware that some very appropriate competitions might have been left out. We hope that readers of this book who know about other contests will let us know, so we can compile even more information for a future edition. In the fourth chapter, we tell you how to get in touch with us, and we hope you do.

How to Use This Book

For every international and national program found in Chapter 2, we again offer specific information in the following four categories: (1) how and where to get information on the program; (2) a description of the program's scope, objectives, and offerings; (3) how to participate and the resources, including time and money, needed to do so; and (4) awards and benefits to be gained from participation.

A related feature of the book is the inclusion of two indexes to help you find appropriate programs. One of the indexes provides a listing by content areas sorted according to level. Obviously, numerous groupings could be used to distinguish the level of competition: primary grades, intermediate grades, middle school, junior high, and senior high. The decision to avoid multiple groupings and use only two groups—elementary and secondary—was based on the fact that the other terms are used with varying frequency, depending on region and interest. The dual classification system is intended to promote ease of use. The competitions and contests grouped and designated as elementary are for students in kindergarten through Grade 6. The secondary group refers to Grades 7–12. Within each program description, you will occasionally see the phrase *junior and senior high* used next to grade level. These terms were used when the contest brochure specified these levels. When the contests were restricted to particular grades, we noted that.

The second index lists the competitions by title in alphabetical order. It will help you find information about programs you may wish to use. You may be looking for something specific or need to refer to a competition that you have already begun to use.

Characteristics of Good Competitions

In light of the many demands on time and money that we all face, it is important to make informed choices regarding contest participation. Obviously, not all competitive activities are equal. When trying to select the best competitions for your own use, it is important to have a set of criteria in mind. Your choice should be based on personal characteristics and goals. A good activity for one student might not be a good choice for another (Feldhusen, Dai, & Clinkenbeard,

2000). Personality traits that may have a bearing include perception of self-worth; ability level; interests; goals; and ability to deal with stress, anxiety, and failure. Beyond personal considerations, the nature of the activity or event is an important issue. For example, the content area (e.g., mathematics, science, or language arts), as well as the age of the student for whom the competition is designed, should be considered. Also, the structure of the process or programmatic features may determine its appropriateness, or at least provide information to consider in the deliberation process. Characteristics to consider include the timeline that is followed; whether it is a team or individual competition; what opportunities for interaction with others are available; and the types of awards offered—cash prizes, plaques, scholarships, and travel.

In selecting the best programs for your purposes, we offer seven general criteria that may be useful. These should be used together to evaluate programs. A low rating on one criterion or the absence of any one of the characteristics does not guarantee that the program is an inferior activity or that it should automatically be eliminated from further consideration. Depending on what you hope to gain from the competition, the absence of one or more of the criteria may not be a problem for you. However, low ratings on several items may be a good basis for not selecting one activity over another. We have not applied these seven criteria to each of the competitions in this book. Our inclusion of a competition does not mean we endorse it. Each of the criteria is discussed below.

Do Students Want to Participate?

Competition entry and participation should be fun. If a contest does not appeal to potential entrants, either skip it or try to figure out why it is not appealing and attempt to change the attitude—but remember, not all competitions are for all people. Some competitions should be passed over because potential entrants are already involved in so many activities that they feel tired or are unable to give sufficient time and effort to another activity. Other reasons for skipping a competition are fear of failure and fear of being in front of a group. These are the types of reasons not only for skipping a competition but also for working to identify the problem and overcome it.

Does The Contest Have a Clearly Stated Purpose?

Unless someone is interested in competition for its own sake, the lack of a stated purpose is probably a basis for elimination from further consideration. If the purpose is stated, then the next step is to evaluate it in light of what one hopes to gain from the activity. Three questions to ask are the following:

1. Is the purpose consistent with my goals and objectives?
2. Is the competition in the correct content area?
3. Does it stress the area(s) of competition I desire?

For example, if someone's interest is in spelling, then a competition in problem solving may be passed up for one in the former academic content area. However, if the person's interest is in public speaking, then something to build problem-solving and reasoning skills might be a good idea. The overriding factor here might not be the goals of the competition but the needs of the individual.

Does the Competition Offer
Resources to Help Participants Prepare?

Unlike the first criterion, a lack of resources is probably not a basis for automatic elimination. In fact, many of the very best contests do indeed offer some kind of assistance. The availability of resources to assist in preparation moves a competition beyond the traditional image. When preparation resources are offered, then the competition is designed not only to provide a competitive environment but also to aid in skills acquisition. The types of resources that may be offered vary widely. Possibilities include the following:

- Sample or practice exercises or problems
- A bibliography of sources from which generally useful information about successful contest strategies can be gained
- A full curriculum
- Lists of study or preparation strategies
- Sources of helpful information, such as motivational and relaxation exercises
- Copies of old tests

Some resources are available on request at no charge. Others are available for a fee, and their circulation may be restricted to school personnel or some other designated group.

Does the Contest Provide
Constructive Feedback on Performance?

Competitive activities can be more than just performance showcases where the best is recognized and the rest are overlooked. The provision of timely, constructive feedback to participants on performance is an asset that some competitions and contests offer. In a sense, all competitions give feedback. For many, this is restricted to information about whether the participant is an award- or prizewinner. The provision of that type of feedback can be interpreted as shifting the emphasis to demonstrating superior performance but not necessarily excellence. The best competitions promote excellence, not just winning or "beating" others. The emphasis on superiority is what we typically see as fostering a detrimental effect of competition. Performance feedback requires that the program go beyond the "win, place, or show" level of feedback. Information about performance can be very helpful, not only to the participant who does not win or place but also to those who do.

Performance feedback is useful in several ways. First, it helps in understanding why one is or is not a winner. Second, it helps to hone skills for later competitions by refining skills and strategies. Third, it facilitates the adjustment of inaccurate perceptions of competence. Fourth, it assists in identifying areas of skill deficit. Feedback also provides guidance for performance in settings outside the specific contest or competition. Finally, it can soften the blow of losing if it lets the participant know that the performance was not all bad and that there were some high-quality features in it.

Participants cannot assume that the feedback will necessarily be glowing and complimentary. The only restrictions are that it should not be degrading or overly critical and that it should be presented in a manner that is easy to interpret and process. It should give accurate information about why one's performance is rated as it is. In some instances, suggestions for improvement are presented. Such information may include the following:

- An estimate of the degree to which the work met the task demands
- Guidelines for better performance
- Samples of model responses that are better
- Strategies to use in the competitive process
- Methods for critiquing or checking one's own work
- An answer key

Unfortunately, it is usually impossible for feedback from competitions and contests to give information about improvement over previous performance and relative ability.

Will Participation Help Students Acquire Skills That Are Applicable Elsewhere?

In addition to their stated purpose, some competitions foster group activity and experience that focus on a long-range goal and working toward it. Through group activity, such skills as cooperation, sharing of resources, collaboration, and other abilities can be acquired and expanded. The availability of such learning opportunities is an extra advantage that may positively influence a decision to participate in a competition. Learning to work in isolation and rely totally on one-self is important, but so is acquiring the ability to participate in a group. In one instance, Ali, a fourth grader, had been participating in a competition called "Future Problem Solving" (FPS) for a year. When he was asked what skills he had learned, he said that he had become a more tolerant person. He then explained that before he had partici-pated in FPS, he had trouble working in groups because he did not believe that others had very good ideas. He preferred to work alone. However, after working with FPS in a team situation, he said that even others' worst ideas gave him ideas he would not have had otherwise.

Furthermore, the competitive process offers the opportunity to focus on a goal that may be accomplished only by hard work over a sustained period of time. Valuable skills related to delayed gratifica-tion and long-range planning may be products that are acquired in the competitive arena and applied elsewhere.

How Easily Can Programmatic Information Be Accessed?

In part, ease of accessibility refers to how widely flyers and brochures are distributed. Access to program officials who are able to provide accurate information, however, may be just as important as availability of printed materials. Being able to contact someone who is knowledgeable for clarification of programmatic procedures, rules, and guidelines can be very important. Potential participants might be able to identify some contests that will be accessible without ever contacting the address given, because they know a school official or member of the sponsoring organization who can assist.

To What Degree Does the Competition Assist Participants in Learning to Consider an Audience?

The need for student products to be reviewed by an authentic audience is essential to the acquisition of many skills. Students may not strive to do their best if all they have to do is prepare work for the teacher to grade. When they know that their work will leave the class-room to be evaluated by some other group, such as contest judges, school boards, local organizations, or newspaper editors, they are more likely to care about refining their work, practicing longer, or get-ting more information. Authentic audiences give bright students a reason to excel—a reason beyond grades. It is also important that par-ticipants be evaluated in a true-to-life manner. Some students set such unrealistic standards for themselves that it may be helpful for them to be evaluated by more realistic criteria. Unreasonable expectations may be more harmful than helpful, and they may be counterproductive to the acquisition of skills.

Learning to consider an audience requires recognizing the multifaceted aspects of an outstanding performance and taking them into consideration in a performance. For instance, the best debater in the world is not likely to do well in a competition if he or she does not speak loudly enough to be heard by the judges. It is easy for competitors to overlook an essential skill if they have never confronted a real audience. Competitors must consider who will read their written products and what criteria these readers will use. Likewise, learning to determine the knowledge base of the audience and adjust one's products accordingly requires practice. It is just as important to learn not to talk down to an audience as it is to avoid talking over their heads.

Reference

Feldhusen, J. F., Dai, D. Y., & Clinkenbeard, P. R. (2000). Dimensions of competitive and cooperative learning among gifted learners. *Journal for the Education of the Gifted, 23,* 328–342.

1

Selecting, Preparing for, and Participating in Competitions

This chapter is designed to help parents, teachers, and others guide students through the process of selecting a competition, preparing for it, and participating in it. We have divided the chapter into four sections:

1. Selected characteristics and needs of gifted and talented students

2. Effects of competition

3. How to anticipate and avoid problems in the use of competitions

4. How to maximize benefits from competitions

In each section, we provide ideas for working with talented students. The focus is on helping students enjoy competition. We offer advice intended to help people who work with students minimize the pressure to win and maximize the intended benefits of each competitive experience. We also provide cautions regarding the use of the programs and specific examples of how to anticipate and avoid problems.

Selected Characteristics and Needs of Gifted and Talented Students: How They Influence Contest Participation

Some Students Are Driven by Their Perfectionism

One area of vulnerability that can plague students, especially highly gifted students, is perfectionism (LoCicero & Ashby, 2000; Schuler, 2000; Silverman, 1999). This can be a heavy burden to bear, because nobody can be perfect. It can also be a double-edged sword. On the one hand, the desire to produce the very best work possible is both noble and worthwhile; on the other hand, it can be stifling if it prohibits production or participation. When perfectionism causes students to avoid embarking on a project or entering a competition for fear of not being perfect, then it is a serious disadvantage. It is not uncommon to find students for whom winning is impossible because of their drive to be perfect. Regardless of what official judges may say, when students are unable to meet their own standards, they will never see themselves as winners. The price this exacts is the loss of joy while going through the process and a missed opportunity to profit from mistakes.

Recent research on perfectionism tells us that this trait may not be all negative. There may be some positive aspects to certain kinds of perfectionism. LoCicero and Ashby (2000) found that gifted students, as compared with a group of their peers in the general cohort, were more adaptive in their perfectionism. This meant that although they were perfectionists, they were not experiencing stress and maladjustment when they did not meet their own standards. Parker (1997) called this a *healthy perfectionist type*. Such students can keep their failures and successes in perspective (Neumeister, 2004b). Neumeister (2004a) found that *self-oriented perfectionists* (i.e., those who set high personal standards for themselves and use these standards to evaluate themselves) believed that a lack of challenge in school contributed to their perfectionism. Therefore, competitions would seem to benefit these students.

The feedback students receive can help them achieve a realistic perspective on their work and level of ability, and the opportunity to interact with others who may be equally capable can offer valuable role models for perfectionists. The personal goal of some competition participants may be to learn that it is important to take competition seriously enough that they do their best and learn from the experience but not so seriously that the objective of the competition, what can be learned, and even their ability to perform at the optimal level, are lost or impaired.

The Need for Challenge May Drive Students Toward Competitions and Contests

As with perfectionists, there are bright students who need to use and expand their special abilities, and gifted students in particular usually deliberately choose to compete. Intellectual challenge can help students gain self-confidence (Glass, 2004) and enhance achievement (Kanevsky & Keighley, 2003) if they display their abilities. Competitive involvement may push them in a way that the regular school curriculum does not (Rotigel & Fello, 2004). One reason for this is the fact that competitive activities may provide an opportunity to interact with intellectual peers or even superiors. This can be a key to the formation of mentor relationships and the establishment of friendships. Second, the competitive process can allow the student to participate in an in-depth study in an area of interest.

Some Students Fall in Love With a Particular Topic at a Very Early Age

School personnel cannot always provide sufficient appropriate opportunities and outlets for talented students. Many of them need outlets for expression beyond the regular education curriculum (Haensly, 2004). Some of these outlets almost certainly have to be outside the classroom and even outside the school. The issue is not simply a matter of teachers not being able to grade enough papers, give enough time for speaking, and devise enough assignments. Some of the outlets need to be things that go beyond the school curriculum. These can include opportunities to meet and interact with other students who have similar interests and to engage in in-depth study beyond the level of the classroom teacher in a specialized interest area.

Students need an authentic audience for their work. Consideration of the audience to which they are speaking, writing, or otherwise presenting a product is crucial. As adults, we often take more care with something when we know it will be read or critiqued. Unfortunately, this is not a skill that students automatically acquire in equal measure to their knowledge and skill levels. They must learn to prepare for others beyond the classroom. The broader knowledge base these students possess requires that they learn to select the information, presentation format, and level on the basis of the audience.

Some Students Have Specific Subject-Matter Aptitude

Many people think of stereotypical talented students as excelling in all areas; however, many of these students might exhibit average ability in most areas but special ability in only one. For example, Milli is in an accelerated mathematics class but working at grade level in all other subject areas. She clearly has special aptitude in mathematics, and competitions offer her an opportunity to demonstrate that and to grow further in that area. One mistaken belief is that when individuals excel in one particular subject area, it is good to pull back instruction in that area and emphasize the areas in which they are less able. Contrary to that belief, gifted students should be allowed to excel in the subject area in which they have special abilities while continuing to receive instruction in other areas. Therefore, students who have shown evidence of current accomplishment in a specific subject should be allowed to work in that area in a more in-depth manner (Lohman, 2005). Competitions are one way to facilitate this.

Effects of Competition: Good News

When considering the effects of competition, one must remember that it is a complex subject. Therefore, there are no simple answers, only factors to weigh in making the best choices for a given student. The first evidence of this comes in defining the concept of competition. There are different interpretations of *competition*, depending on the situation and the person to whom you are talking. The term typically is used to refer to the rivalry between two or more persons for a single goal or prize. This means that if one person wins, then the other does not win. However, the internal competition one experiences while striving against the self and prior accomplishments is also referred to as a form of competition by some. Unlike the first situation, internal competition allows a person to win if he or she meets a self-imposed goal, regardless of the performance of others. For the purposes of this discussion, the first definition—rivalry in trying to achieve a goal—is used. Beyond that basic issue, competitive experiences are usually discussed in terms of a single structured environment where an activity takes place. Examples of these kinds of competitions are a spelling bee and a timed math competition. Participants come together for the purpose of competition. They demonstrate their competence in the context of specific restrictions and rules (time limits, resource guidelines, etc.).

However, this image does not apply to all the competitions we discuss in this book. Many of the contests described in Chapter 2 and listed in the indexes require the submission of a product that is then evaluated. The product is developed and evaluated according to a set of criteria. Because the evaluation of the products occurs only in a single, structured environment, such a competition does not fit the traditional image of a competitive event. The preparation of the product, invention, or paper usually is done at the participants' pace outside of the evaluation environment. Even though participants must follow contest guidelines, there may not be time limits or other similar restrictions. Because of these and other variations, the degree to which the negative and positive effects of competition are realized varies. Positive effects of competition may include the following:

Competition Prepares Participants for the Competitive Nature of School and Society

Although talented students may have an edge over other students in terms of ability to acquire academic subject matter—history, mathematics, spelling, and so on—such students may not have any advantage in dealing with the characteristics of a competitive situation. In fact, their ability to demonstrate their excellence in some areas may be hampered by their limited skill in dealing with competition. Having numerous opportunities to be involved in competitive settings may help them learn to function effectively in competitive settings and to develop feelings of competence (Bumpus, Olbeter, & Glover, 1998). People performing alone on simple tasks do well, but with complex ones they perform better in the presence of other people (Guerin, 2003). In one study, girls saw competition as a chance to encourage others to do well (Rizza & Reis, 2001). The more times they have the experience, the better they can become at coping with failure, managing both positive and negative feelings, and operating within the constraints of competitive situations. To be successful, students must follow instructions and manage time; however, some students may perform at or below average on these needed skills. The high level of creativity some students exhibit is an asset, unless they fail to recognize the importance of channeling this in specific situations so that superior ability can be demonstrated. Likewise, intense concentration and an unusually long attention span are assets, unless they interfere with the student's compliance with time constraints. In-depth knowledge is an asset if participants can discipline themselves to ensure that the most important information is presented, even if some of the trivial information is omitted.

Competition Provides Feedback on the Relative Standing of One's Performance

This principle may be particularly important for students who need the opportunity to assess just how superior their abilities are to those of others. The best math students in a given school may find that they are only slightly above average compared with all other math students in a region or state. It is better to find this out early than to wait until college to suddenly learn that there are other very bright people out there. In a recent study, some students did express the need to take part in competitions to determine their comparison to others. This information motivated self-improvement (Feldhusen, Dai, & Clinkenbeard, 2000). In addition, participation in competition can help students understand their strengths and weaknesses and learn coping skills if they lose the competition (Stormont, Stebbins, & Holliday, 2001).

One component of the feedback process may be the unique opportunity for students to work with other people of equal ability. Students may find that they are far superior to others. Although test scores are reported with the results of standardized achievement tests, it may not be sufficient in helping students understand and recognize their ability. Someone who is the most outstanding student in his or her daily environment might have difficulty comprehending that he or she is or is not the most accomplished student in the world, state, or city. Learning early that many others out there are equally bright as oneself is helpful in recognizing the importance of doing one's best and respecting the abilities of others.

Competition Can Focus Attention on a Specific Content Area, Problem, Task, or Strategy and Consequently Enable Participants to Hone a Set of Specific Skills

This may be a particular advantage for some students who are typically so successful in many different content areas that they never really engage in in-depth study in any one area. The competition may serve as a basis for the desire and need to focus on one content area. Even if the focus is not permanent, a number of skills will likely be acquired that will be applicable in other content areas and life situations. Likewise, the information gained from the in-depth emphasis on one area may have application in others. To illustrate, Eric took part in a creative writing contest sponsored by a well-known magazine. He learned how to develop a storyline and create rich characters for his contest entry. Later, he demonstrated these skills in both language arts classes and speech classes. Competition can help students refine and develop talent (Riley & Karnes, 2005).

Competition May Stimulate Increased Interest in the Task or Content Area

Here is another example: To prepare for a contest, Madison had to do a lot of reading and studying about the American Revolution. Prior to that, she had always made good grades in history classes but had no particular interest in the subject. As she became immersed in the American Revolution, her interest in history in general and in that specific topic began to grow. Equally as important as her interest in the subject was that her ability to analyze and synthesize what she was reading began to expand and transfer to other subjects. Gradually, she began to ask questions that moved her learning forward more rapidly than before. Students who take part in content-area competitions just might fall in love with that area or with some aspect of it.

Competition Enhances Achievement, Motivation, and Productivity

This is sometimes true for learning tasks that are highly structured. The drill that is often associated with the acquisition of basic skills can be enhanced by competition. Therefore, the acquisition of math facts and concepts, spelling words, and grammar rules may really profit from the competitive process. In any content area, there are principles, rules, and other similar information that has to be learned if the student is to progress to higher levels. The other side of this advantage is discussed in terms of competition's failure to promote problem solving, critical thinking, and other learning strategies. However, in many of the competitions discussed in Chapter 2, this is not a limitation. Complex strategies are fostered in many competitions we describe.

In addition, if the competitor perceives the competition as a means of learning and striving for one's personal best, then competing can facilitate learning (Feldhusen et al., 2000; Tauer & Harackiewicz, 2004) and even performance (Stanne, Johnson, & Johnson, 1999) and motivation (Tauer & Harackiewicz, 2004). Competitors, as opposed to those who do not compete, can also increase what is called *competence valuation*, which involves placing importance on doing well. If one does place importance on doing well, then this enhances the meaningfulness of the participation, and winning enhances feelings of competence (Reeve & Deci, 1996).

Working in Small Groups in Competitions Produces Other Benefits for Students

Many organizations and businesses currently depend on the work of small groups to be productive and reach their goals (Mulvey & Ribbens, 1999). We know that interpersonal competitions can increase individual performance (Mulvey & Ribbens, 1999). Recent evidence has now shown that working in small groups of fewer than about ten members produces beneficial effects. If students combine cooperation in the small group with intergroup competition, then this group working on a common goal can expect little or no negative effects of competition, and if, while cooperating, these small groups divide tasks, they will be even more efficient (Tauer & Harackiewicz, 2004). These small groups who work together as opposed to those who do not cooperate have been shown to have higher productivity, more efficiency, more ambitious group goals, and higher group efficacy (Mulvey & Ribbens, 1999). This efficacy means they believe they can do well and succeed.

Effects of Competition: Bad News

As a Result of Competition, Individuals Can Adopt an Egoistic, Ability-Focused, and External Motivational Orientation

Despite the purported advantages of competition, it is not without problems. The main achievement goal can become outperforming others. Self-worth may become tied to winning or at least to doing better than others. Unfortunately, when students cannot demonstrate superior achievement, their self-worth can suffer. In short, they might think that they are valuable because of the superior achievement, not because of other, innate qualities. The goal adults have for most students is that they act with what is called *intrinsic motivation*. This motivation allows students to participate in activities for the love of learning and the satisfaction of taking part in the activity in the absence of reward or punishment (Deci, 1975). If students are pressured to win, then they might experience a negative effect on intrinsic motivation, especially if they lose the competition (Bumpus et al., 1998; Reeve & Deci, 1996). Fortunately, most gifted and talented students perceive themselves as more competent and intrinsically motivated than others, but this should still be protected (Vallerand, Gagne, Senecal, & Pelletier, 1994).

Competition Might Drive the Need to Demonstrate Superior Achievement by Avoiding the Risk of Failure

The need to win may cause students to avoid the most difficult or complex task in favor of an easier one that they can win (Dai & Feldhusen, 1998). Their aspirations may be lowered, and there may be increased indifference toward excellence and intrinsic motivation. The desire to experience perceived success could restrict the drive to work at the upper limits of one's potential. This can be a serious problem in and of itself, but its implications are even more significant if they are considered in light of the long-term effect that lowered intrinsic motivation will have: The student loses the desire to do the best job possible and strive for excellence. Many things people do in school and life they do because they are intrinsically motivated and because external rewards frequently are not available. If, instead of doing one's best, one does just enough to outperform others, what happens when there are no others against whom to compete and measure oneself? For talented students, the discrepancy between what may be enough to guarantee success and what may be needed to function at one's upper limits may be great.

Success and Failure Can Come to Be Viewed as the Result of Ability Alone Rather Than Effort and Motivation

It is important to avoid this view. In reality, superior achievement is usually the result of a combination of ability, hard work, and drive. Ability without motivation and work frequently will not get students very far. An attitude that fails to recognize the importance of all three factors may hamper students' learning. Even though gifted and talented young people can learn more than other learners, they must work to reach their potential. Experiencing success primarily as a means of establishing high perceived ability may reduce the likelihood that students will achieve at their level of ability.

Competition Does Not Appear to Enhance Performance on Problem-Solving or Creative Tasks

The issue here is not whether there is a competitive process but rather what the guidelines of the competition are. Competitions that require the creation of new ideas and thinking processes certainly cannot be faulted for having this disadvantage. Such competitions evaluate the analysis and synthesis of information rather than rote application of facts. They can be shown to help in problem solving and creativity (Tallent-Runnels, 1993; Tallent-Runnels & Yarbrough, 1992).

How to Anticipate and Avoid Problems in the Use of Competitions

As students approach the competitive process in general or a specific competition, some problems can be identified ahead of time and minimized. One of the ever-present problems is deficiencies in time management and test-taking skills. The assumption that because students are talented they are good at taking tests and managing time is false (Tallent-Runnels et al., 1994). The problem may surface or be most evident during the period of preparation for the competition or during the competition itself. Participants who work too slowly, waste time, or do not schedule time appropriately will not be successful in competition, regardless of how much knowledge or skill they are capable of demonstrating. To avoid or minimize time management problems, work with students on time management strategies as well as on ways to truly benefit from competitions. Some specific helpful things you can do include the following:

Conduct a Mock Test-Taking Session Using Time Limits

For example, if the competition will require students to answer four questions from a group of seven in four hours, they must answer each question in one hour, on average. Students who take one hour and twenty minutes for each of the first three questions will run out of time before answering the fourth and final one. This time management problem could cost students the competition. To avoid this, you might structure practice testing sessions in which the student must select one question from among three and respond to it in one hour.

If the Competition Requires Preparation of a Product for Submission (a Speech, Research Project, Invention, Essay, etc.), Help Students Organize the Study or Training Required Prior to Entry

It may be helpful to have students develop a realistic schedule for meeting the demand in a timely manner. This requires that you consider all the other activities in which students are involved and then schedule a work period for this added project. This means you must be realistic about the other demands on the students' time; also, it may require you to consider the schedules of others, something many of us fail to do.

Once Students Embark on the Schedule, Make Sure They Reevaluate It to See If it Is Working

The only way to determine whether a schedule is realistic is to use it for a while. After a week or so, ask the following questions:

Are you able to maintain the schedule?

If you maintain the schedule, will you be ready for the competition deadline?

If the answer to either of these questions is no, then the schedule needs to be adjusted.

When Scheduling Periods of Preparation, Suggest That Students Think in Terms of the Amount of Work to Be Completed or Studied, Rather Than the Specified Amount of Time to Use

For example, if there are 6,000 words to study for a spelling contest that is six weeks away, then the student will need to study a minimum of 1,000 words per week. That figure can be divided further to establish an exact number per day.

When Tackling a Task, Suggest That Students Examine the Total Picture and Then Make Some Informed Decisions

For instance, in the spelling contest example provided above, whether the words on the list are all unfamiliar to the student, or a combination of familiar and unfamiliar words, makes a lot of difference. If some of the words are familiar, then they may be removed from the list of words to study. Perhaps there are only 2,398 that require study. That is a much more manageable task than studying 6,000 words.

Teach Students the Most Effective Strategies for Taking Tests, So They Are Able to Make Informed Choices and the Best Decisions About Guessing and Other Response Techniques

The following are some strategies for students to consider as they take part in competitions:

1. *Answer the questions you know first and skip any question you cannot answer.* There are several reasons for this. First, the answer to a question may be found later in the test, or it may just pop into your mind. Second, sitting and trying to think of an answer that may or may not come to you may be a waste of valuable time. Furthermore, the longer you stare at the one(s) you do not know, the less confident and more stressed and anxious you may become. Anxiety keeps you from doing your best. Move on and build your confidence.

2. *On true/false and multiple-choice tests, remember that questions that include "absolute" words, such as* all, always, *and* never, *are almost certainly false.* Very seldom is there an exception to this rule.

3. *On true/false and multiple-choice questions, words that you have never seen before may be an indication that this answer does not belong; therefore, it is not the correct answer.*

4. *On true/false and multiple-choice questions, numbers and dates that are too high or low, or out of the range of other possible answer choices, may be wrong.*

5. *If time allows, once you finish the test, check your work for completeness and accuracy.* If you find questions that were skipped earlier, try to answer them. If you think an answer is incorrect, think twice before you change it. Unless you are positive that the answer is wrong, do not change it. Your first response is usually the right one.

6. *Practice possible outline techniques.* Although a student probably will not have time to use traditional outline strategies, it may be helpful to make a list of references to cite, dates to mention, or key terms to include in the answers on an upcoming test.

7. *Take an opportunity to view examples of good and bad responses.* If you have the test questions from a previous year, you can construct sample responses to critique. Having the chance to look at an answer that may not be perfect, but could be acceptable, can be a good way to emphasize what is and is not considered in grading, things to watch for and try to avoid, and possible response formats.

8. *Discuss the meaning of and practice using the key words and terms that are often critical to responding correctly to a test question.* These terms include *compare and contrast, criticize, illustrate, justify, prove,* and *synthesize.*

9. *Help participants focus on the objectives of the competition.*

Some very capable and accomplished participants do not do well in a competition because they fail to recognize or consider its purpose. For entrants who are unaffected by a lack of recognition, or even by failure, this may not be a problem. However, the real purpose of competitive activity should be to enjoy doing the best possible job of achieving the goal of the competition. To maximize focus on the objectives, discuss the purpose of the competition with students. In addition to whatever stated goals and objectives you may know, look for other sources of information to include. The evaluation criteria and preparation resources may be helpful in the discussion. In part, this is the idea of learning to interpret and follow the rules. However, it also involves developing the ability to adjust one's knowledge and skills to a stated goal or objective. The most successful participants adjust their work to their audience.

Let Students Know That Their Self-Worth and Self-Esteem Should Not Be Determined by the Level of Performance in Competition

Winning should not be the sole purpose of participating in a competition. The goal of the competitive process should be to gain experience and knowledge and enjoy the activity. For students whose self-worth is too tied in with superior achievement, the following suggestions may be helpful:

- Devote time and effort to helping students recognize the other purposes of the competition and how those fit into personal goals and objectives.
- Help students work on realizing that the value of the individual is innate. One's worth is not based solely on accomplishments or the outcome of a particular competition.
- Remind students that winning is not a goal to prove superiority over others but a means to test their own competence (Bumpus et al., 1998).
- Build recognition that the top winners in many competitions may have competed for several years before they won.
- Be sure that feedback is informational and not considered controlling (Bumpus et al., 1998).

For example, the first year that Rachel entered a spelling competition, she won at the local level but lost in the fifth round at the district level. The next year, she won at both the local and district levels but was eliminated in the ninth round at the regional level. Finally, in the third year, she progressed to the national level of competition and won. This steady progression is frequently omitted from discussions of winning.

Help Students Whose Low Self-Worth Prohibits Their Participation in Competitive Activities or Greatly Diminishes Their Ability to Perform

With these students, use some of the anxiety- and stress-reduction techniques discussed earlier. Working on the time management and test-taking skills mentioned earlier also can help move students in the right direction. If possible, take advantage of repeated competition participation as a means of helping students learn from mistakes. Depending on how willing students are to become involved in national and regional competitions, local events, many of which will take place in a classroom setting, may be appropriate. To do this, there must be evidence of relative progress on a set of criteria. For example, in competitions that provide feedback, students may be able to chart their growth. In conditions that do not provide feedback, and in circumstances where students are not participating in a competition that has the same evaluative criteria, this is difficult. To foster this kind of understanding and recognition, have students set some goals or guidelines for assessing their performance that are not directly related to any one competition. After each participation, have them use those criteria to evaluate their personal performance and develop ways to improve. Work to attribute these students' success to factors such as ability and to attribute failure to lack of effort.

Gifted or talented students' exceptional ability may not extend to skill in working with others and to value their work. In a few cases, the problem may be a lack of appropriate social skills. If that is true, then it is helpful to teach students ways to interact socially. This typically is not the situation; instead, there is a need to learn to use the group process to maximize potential. Potential participants may find it helpful to practice working in groups and taking and giving constructive feedback. There are techniques for group problem solving and brainstorming that can be learned prior to any competition. Likewise, developing and learning strategies for dividing up tasks and assigning responsibilities can be helpful. Finally, discussing the value of the contributions of others can be helpful.

Help Students Deal With the Pressure of Competition

For some students, the nervousness and anxiety that competition brings impair their ability to perform at the optimal level. Students can use these strategies:

- Use relaxation exercises.
- Practice focusing attention on the task at hand and excluding the anxiety-provoking characteristics of the situation.

This includes learning to ignore other test-takers. In most contests, speed is not the primary issue; accuracy and quality are. Thus, students should learn that the first person to finish does not automatically have any better chance of winning than the last person to finish.

How to Maximize Benefits From Competitions

Beyond the things that can be done to prepare students for competition and minimize the potential problems, a step that must not be overlooked is helping students to maximize the benefits of the competitive experience. Ways to accomplish this include the following:

- Making a list of what they have learned academically, socially, and personally
- Discussing what they have learned to ensure they recognize that, in addition to skills and techniques, insights resulting from the analysis and synthesis of information also are acquired
- Identifying subject areas where the things that were learned can be applied and examining the resultant benefits of that application; analyzing feedback from the competition and identifying things that need to be done in preparation for the next competition
- Demonstrating transfer applications of processes (use of study skills, group interaction techniques, problem-solving strategies, etc.)
- Formulating a set of goals based on identified needs and devising a schedule for accomplishing them

References

Bumpus, M. A., Olbeter, S., & Glover, S. H. (1998). Influences of situational characteristics on intrinsic motivation. *Journal of Psychology, 132,* 451–463.

Dai, D. Y., & Feldhusen, J. F. (1998). A validation study of the Thinking Styles Inventory: Implications for gifted education. *Roeper Review, 21,* 302–307.

Deci, E. L. (1975). *Intrinsic motivation.* New York: Plenum.

Feldhusen, J. F., Dai, D. Y., & Clinkenbeard, P. R. (2000). Dimensions of competitive and cooperative learning among gifted learners. *Journal for the Education of the Gifted, 23,* 328–342.

Glass, T. F. (2004). What gift? The reality of the student who is gifted and talented in public school classrooms. *Gifted Child Today, 27*(4), 25–29.

Guerin, B. (2003). Social behaviors as determined by different arrangements of social consequences: Diffusion of responsibility effects with competition. *Journal of Social Psychology, 143,* 313–329.

Haensly, P. (2004). Spirit and opportunity: Re-exploring giftedness and parents' expanding directive role. *Gifted Child Today, 27*(4), 40–43.

Kanevsky, L., & Keighley, T. (2003). To produce or not to produce? Understanding boredom and the honor in underachievement. *Roeper Review, 26,* 20–28.

LoCicero, K. A., & Ashby, J. S. (2000). Multidimensional perfectionism in middle school age gifted students: A comparison to peers from the general cohort. *Roeper Review, 22,* 1182–1186.

Lohman, D. F. (2005). An aptitude perspective on talent: Implications for identification of academically gifted minority students. *Journal for the Education of the Gifted, 28,* 333–360.

Mulvey, P. W., Ribbens, B. A. (1999). The effects of intergroup competition and assigned group goals on group efficacy and group effectiveness. *Small Group Research, 30,* 651–657.

Neumeister, K. L. S. (2004a). Factors influencing the development of perfectionism in gifted college students. *Gifted Child Quarterly, 48,* 259–274.

Neumeister, K. L. S. (2004b). Interpreting successes and failures: The influence of perfectionism on perspective. *Journal for the Education of the Gifted, 27,* 311–335.

Parker, W. D. (1997). An empirical typology of perfectionism in academically talented children. *American Educational Research Journal, 34,* 545–562.

Reeve, J., & Deci, E. (1996). Elements of the competitive situation that affect intrinsic motivation. *Personality and Social Psychology Bulletin, 22,* 24–33.

Riley, T. L., & Karnes, F. A. (2005). Problem-solving competitions: Just the solution. *Gifted Child Today, 28*(4), 31–37, 64.

Rizza, M. G., & Reis, S. M. (2001). Comparing and contrasting: Stories of competition. *Gifted Child Quarterly, 45,* 54–62.

Rotigel, J. V., & Fello, S. (2004). Mathematically gifted students: How can we meet their needs? *Gifted Child Today, 27*(4), 46–51.

Schuler, P. A. (2000). Perfectionism and the gifted adolescent. *Journal of Secondary Gifted Education, 11,* 183–196.

Silverman, L. K. (1999). Perfectionism: The crucible of giftedness. *Advanced Development Journal, 8,* 47–61.

Stanne, M., Johnson, D., & Johnson, R. (1999). Does competition enhance or inhibit motor performance: A meta-analysis. *Psychological Bulletin, 125,* 133–154.

Stormont, M., Stebbins, M. S., & Holliday, G. (2001). Characteristics and educational support needs of underrepresented gifted adolescents. *Psychology in the Schools, 38,* 413–423.

Tallent-Runnels, M. K. (1993). The future problem solving program: An investigation of effects on problem solving ability. *Contemporary Educational Psychology, 18,* 382–388.

Tallent-Runnels, M. K., Olivarez, A., Jr., Candler-Lotven, A. C., Walsh, S., Gray, A., & Irons, T. (1994). A comparison of learning and study strategies of gifted and average ability junior high students. *Journal for the Education of the Gifted, 17,* 143–160.

Tallent-Runnels, M. K., & Yarbrough, D. W. (1992). Effects of the future problem solving program on children's concerns about the future. *Gifted Child Quarterly, 4,* 190–194.

Tauer, J. M., & Harackiewicz, J. M. (2004). The effects of cooperation and competition on intrinsic motivation and performance. *Journal of Personality and Social Psychology, 86,* 849–861.

Vallerand, R. J., Gagne, F., Senecal, C., & Pelletier, L. G. (1994). A comparison of the school intrinsic motivation and perceived competence of gifted and regular students. *Gifted Child Quarterly, 38,* 172–175.

2

Competition Descriptions

In this chapter, you will find information on 165 competitions that are available to children and youth from kindergarten to Grade 12. We have provided information on each competition; indexes at the end of this book will help you find competitions to suit your goals. The competitions in this chapter are listed by title in alphabetical order. For each competition, you will find information under the following headings:

Contact: Specific names of individuals or names of the organizations to contact are listed first, after the competition title. We listed as much information as we could find in order to make it easy for you to obtain information on the contest. In some cases, no traditional contact information was available, and for those competitions only the Web site is listed.

Web Site: The specific electronic address for each competition

Description: Goals of the competition. If we could not determine the goal on the basis of the literature we reviewed, we simply described what the competition requires students to do.

How to Participate: How to enter the competition and/or how to get more information. For some contests, this can be as detailed as offering information for every level or category of entry.

Cost: Sometimes these are per person or team, and sometimes they are per school or district.

Categories/Content Areas: Some contests focus on categories within content areas, such as poetry or prose within Language Arts. Content areas used to describe the competitions are as follows: Computers, Drama, Foreign Language, General Problem Solving, Language Arts, Mathematics, Science, Social Studies, and Speech.

Ages/Grade Levels: The ages specified by the contest organizers or the grades that can enter the contests. Sometimes contest organizers will list only levels, such as elementary, junior high, or senior high.

Status: This tells you whether the competition is *regional*, which means open to a certain number of states in a region. You will find only a few regional competitions in this book. You will also find many that are considered national and are also open to students in Department of Defense schools outside of the United States. In addition, many of the competitions are offered on an international basis.

Time Commitment: How much time competitors must devote to the competition. In some cases, contest information revealed that only a certain number of hours or class periods were involved. In other cases, estimation of time is much more difficult and depends on many factors, including the skills and styles of the competitors. In those cases, we tried to offer some clues to time commitment.

Resources Needed: What contest organizers provide to help you prepare. The section also describes resources that you must have to participate.

Awards/Benefits: These vary from contest to contest. We listed information about certificates, money, and other awards that go to winners and others who do well in the competitions. For some competitions, we also listed academic and personal benefits that participants can derive from competing, as they were described by the contest organizers.

The first index that might help you find a particular program is the Index of Competitions by Title, found on pages 152–157. To find competitions in specific content areas, consult the Index of Competitions by Subject Area and Level, on pages 158–169. Here you will also find the content areas listed by level—elementary or secondary.

AAA High School Travel Challenge

Contact: aaatravelchallenge@national.aaa.com
Web Site: http://www.aaa.com
Description: The American Automobile Association (AAA) High School Travel Challenge aims to reward students for their travel knowledge. The contest encourages interest in travel, tourism, and careers in hospitality while improving students' geographic vocabulary.
How to Participate: Online participation begins in December. Participants must register, read the rules and regulations, and take a practice online test to make sure they meet the personal computer and Internet

browser requirements to compete in January. The online competition is in January, and students will complete a timed, online examination consisting of forty randomly selected questions. The top five scorers in each state will then compete in a state competition, where they will be given a written, proctored exam. The top scorers will be designated *state champions*. The state champion in each state and the District of Columbia will advance to the national competition in Orlando, Florida, which takes place in May.

The top five scorers who are registered for "travel-specific" scholarships will be asked to submit an essay to be judged by a panel of judges. One winner in each state and the District of Columbia will receive a travel-specific award of $1,000 and will be entered in a national level of competition where the winner will receive an additional $5,000 scholarship.

Cost: None

Categories/Content Areas: Geography

Ages/Grade Levels: Grades 9–12; public, private, and home-schooled students

Status: National

Time Commitment: Online registration begins in December, and the online contest takes place in early to mid-January. Students who qualify compete in the state competition, which takes place in early March. The top scorers compete in the national competition in May in Orlando.

Resources Needed: Participants must register, complete an online practice examination, and meet minimum personal computer and Internet browser standards.

Awards/Benefits: Participants compete for more than $100,000 in scholarships and great prizes. Top scorers in each state will receive a free trip for the competitor and a parent or guardian for the national competition in Orlando. There are two types of scholarships available: (1) *unrestricted* awards, for students with skills in travel trivia and geography, and (2) *travel-specific* awards, for students with an interest in careers in the travel and tourism industry. Students can be eligible for both.

AATSP Elementary/Middle School Poster Contest

Contact: AATSP (American Association of Teachers of Spanish and Portuguese), 523 Exton Commons, Exton, PA 19341-2451. Phone: 610-363-7005. Fax: 610-363-7116. E-mail: corporate@aatsp.org

Web Site: http://www.aatsp.org

Description: Participants develop posters around an annual theme.

How to Participate: By the deadline, submit a student information form for each entry to: Colleen DeFouw, Kettle Moraine Middle School, 301 East Ottawa Ave., Dousman, WI 53018. Phone: 262-965-6500, Extension 445. Home phone: 262-264-0647. Fax: 262-965-6506. E-mail: defouwc@kmsd.edu.

Cost: No registration fee

Categories/Content Areas: Foreign Language—Spanish and Portuguese

Ages/Grade Levels: Three categories: Grades K–3, Grades 4–5, and Grades 6–8

Status: National

Time Commitment: The time required to write an essay; varies from entrant to entrant

Resources Needed: Entry form and poster materials

Awards/Benefits: First, second, and third prizes are awarded in each grade category. Each entrant receives a certificate.

Academic Games Leagues of America National Tournament

Contact: Academic Games Leagues of America, Inc.; P.O. Box 17563; West Palm Beach, FL 33406.

Web Site: http://www.academicgames.org

Description: This competition aims to challenge and reward outstanding knowledge and performance in mathematics, language arts, and social studies.

How to Participate: Participants qualify for the national tournament through local leagues. National tournament registration forms can be found on the Web site listed above. Participants compete in teams of five.

Cost: There is a $75 registration fee per person. National participants must bear the costs of attending the competition.

Categories/Content Areas: Mathematics/Language Arts/Social Studies

Ages/Grade Levels: Grades 4–12

Status: National

Time Commitment: The national tournament takes place in April. Registration begins in January and varies with local leagues.

Resources Needed: A local league, team of five participants, entry fees, registration forms

Awards/Benefits: Local and national awards vary by year and location. Participants can visit the Web site each year for specific awards.

Academic Triathlon

Contact: Peggy L. Sheldon, U.S Academic Triathlon National Coordinator, P.O. Box 1765, Minnetonka, MN 55345. Phone: 952-934-1438. E-mail: homeofusat@aol.com.

Web Site: http://www.academictriathlon.org

Description: The Academic Triathlon is a series of three meets: (1) PARTY (Preparation, Assembly, and Reenactment Theater is Yours) in a Box, (2) Face-Off, and (3) Mind Sprints. In PARTY in a Box, teams receive a problem and equipment with which to solve it within a set time frame. In the Face-Off, teams answer questions on an array of academic content areas, current events, and consumer issues. In the Mind Sprints, teams solve problems. Teams are composed of five students. Fifth- and sixth-grade teams compete against each other, and seventh- and eighth-grade teams compete against each other, to answer grade-appropriate questions. The best total score for the three events wins. Teams accumulate grand total scores in three round-robin meets.

How to Participate: Follow the registration guidelines. Team registration fees cover the cost of the materials and secure sets of questions and the physical setup necessary for a smooth-running Academic Triathlon. The Academic Triathlon is a "turn-key" operation, with everything required for meets shipped in advance.

Cost: $225 for the first team, $195 for each additional team. Training videotapes are $25 each. The program manual, schedules, databases, and meet forms are available in a downloadable format on the Web site listed above.

Categories/Content Areas: Critical/Divergent Thinking, Team Building, Cooperation, Creative and Performing Arts/Language Arts

Ages/Grade Levels: Grades 5–8

Status: Local, regional, state

Time Commitment: Competitions are scheduled each month, and schedules are published in the monthly newsletter. Each meet lasts three hours. Teams may prepare as much or as little as student and adviser time permits.

Resources Needed: Entry form, kit, and official questions

Awards/Benefits: Ribbons are given for placing in the round-robin and regional events, and all students receive participation certificates. First-, second-, and third-place winners at regional and state events receive achievement awards. Creativity certificates can be awarded at any meet.

Achievement Awards in Writing

Contact: NCTE (National Council of Teachers of English), 1111 W. Kenyon Rd., Urbana, IL 61801-1096. Phone: 800-369-NCTE (800-369-6283) and 217-328-3870. Fax: 217-328-0977.

Web Site: http://www.ncte.org

Description: For this competition, nominees submit two written compositions: (1) an impromptu theme on a topic designated by the NCTE and (2) a writing sample (prose or verse). The first is written under teacher supervision in no more than two hours. Research papers, term papers, or novels do not qualify for the latter. The writing sample may not exceed ten typed, double-spaced pages.

How to Participate: For each school nominee, submit an official nomination form that is postmarked no later than the specified deadline (near February 1).

Cost: None

Categories/Content Areas: Composition/Language Arts

Ages/Grade Levels: Juniors in high school

Status: United States and Canada, as well as American schools abroad

Time Commitment: Deadlines are as follows:

Late January/early February: Deadline for schools to return nomination blanks

March: Impromptu themes topic and further instructions are sent to teachers

Late April: Deadline for teachers to mail nominees' impromptu themes and best writing samples to state coordinators

August: State coordinators report results to NCTE

October: NCTE announces the awards

Resources Needed: Official nomination form, which can be obtained from NCTE

Awards/Benefits: Each state may have up to two winners for each seat in the U.S. House of Representatives allotted to the state. The District of Columbia and Canada are allowed four winners, and the American schools abroad are allowed two winners. Award recipients and the English departments that nominated them receive certificates of commendation.

NCTE does not award scholarships; however, names and addresses of winners are published in a booklet that NTCE mails to directors of admissions and freshman studies at colleges, universities, and junior colleges in the United States. Accompanying each booklet is a letter in which NCTE recommends the winners for college admission and for financial assistance, if needed.

In collaboration with the Scholastic Writing Awards, NCTE Achievement Award recipients are offered the option of having the sample of their best work submitted to the Scholastic Writing Awards.

Alliance for Young Artists and Writers Scholastic Art and Writing Awards

Web Site: http://www.scholastic.com
Description: This competition evaluates writing and art in a variety of categories.
How to Participate: Participants submit creative works of art and fiction to local affiliates. Participants can enter creative works in a number of categories listed on the Web site given above. Students begin the submission process by registering online.
Cost: None
Categories/Content Areas: Language Arts/Visual Arts
Ages/Grade Levels: Grades 7–12
Status: United States and Canada
Time Commitment: Varies; submission deadlines also vary on the basis of the local affiliate.
Resources Needed: Registration form, which can be found online; teacher/sponsor; local affiliate
Awards/Benefits: Regional-level winners receive lapel pins and certificates. National-level winners receive medals and certificates and are listed in a national catalogue and on the Web site. Varying amounts of scholarships are awarded to winning high school graduating seniors.

All-USA High School Academic Team Competition

Contact: *USA Today*, 7950 Jones Branch Dr., McLean, VA 22108.
Web Site: http://www.usatoday.com
Description: This program aims to recognize the academic achievements of graduating high school seniors. It recognizes academic achievement and artistic and leadership endeavors.
How to Participate: Nomination forms are available in December and are mailed to principals and guidance directors, or they can be requested by a sponsor.
Cost: None
Categories/Content Areas: Academic Achievement/Leadership/ Language Arts/Visual Arts
Ages/Grade Levels: Graduating/Grade 12 students
Status: National
Time Commitment: Forms are due in February. Teams are selected and announced in May.
Resources Needed: Nomination form and letters of recommendation
Awards/Benefits: The twenty students chosen as representatives will be featured in a two-page spread in *USA Today*. The newspaper will list

the students' accomplishments and pictures. Winners will also receive a trophy and a $2,500 cash award.

Amateur Poetry Contest

Contact: Pen Pushers Publications; Contest CSC-154; 4631 Northwest 31st Ave., Ste. 147; Fort Lauderdale, FL 33309.
Web Site: http://www.poetrycontest.com
Description: This poetry contest is designed for amateur poets. Any style poetry is accepted, including freestyle, lyric, haiku, narrative, limerick, ballads, or dramatic.
How to Participate: Anyone can enter this contest by writing one poem of any style, twenty lines or fewer. Poems are to be submitted to the Web site or mailed to the address listed above.
Cost: None
Categories/Content Areas: Poetry
Ages/Grade Levels: All
Status: International
Time Commitment: Varies. Awards are given out monthly.
Resources Needed: Entry form, which can be found online.
Awards/Benefits: Each month, a grand prize winner is announced. He or she is awarded a $1,000 prize. In addition, twenty-four first prizes of solid gold medals and seventy-nine second-prize bronze medals are given. An annual grand prize of $10,000 is also awarded. Every prize winner has his or her poem published.

American Computer Science League

Contact: American Computer Science League, P.O. Box 521, West Warwick, RI 02893.
Web Site: http://www.acsl.org
Description: The American Computer Science League conducts science and computer programming contests for students in Grades 6–12. Students are given questions and a practical problem to solve in three days. In addition, an invitational all-star contest is held at the end of the year.
How to Participate: Schools may begin to register in July and should register no later than December 1. The registration flyer is posted on the Web site listed above.
Cost: One team, $125; two teams, $225; three teams, $300; four teams, $350
Categories/Content Areas: Science/Computer Science
Ages/Grade Levels: Junior and senior high school students
Status: International

Time Commitment: Contests are held in December, February, March, and April. Preparation time varies; the contest takes three days.
Resources Needed: Registration forms, computers at the team's school to complete the problem, and three days to complete the contest
Awards/Benefits: Trophies and computer equipment

American Enterprise Speech Contest

Contact: American Enterprise Speech Contest, 2210 Arbor Blvd., Dayton, OH 45439-1580. Phone: 937-294-0421. E-mail: nma@nma1.org, martha@nma1.org.
Web Site: http://www.nma1.us
Description: This is a speech contest designed for high school seniors. The speeches must adhere to the general topic "American Competitive Enterprise." The contest aims to promote a greater understanding of the role of economics in free society and to develop students' communication skills.
How to Participate: Participants must first compete in area- and council-level contests before being selected to participate in the finals at the national conference. Chapters wishing to participate must submit a Chapter Confirmation Form. Students' speeches are judged on content, delivery, and language.
Cost: None
Categories/Content Areas: Speech
Ages/Grade Levels: Grades 9–12
Status: National
Time Commitment: The first level of competition is at the chapter level and is typically conducted between January and March.
Resources Needed: Speech contest entry form and a local National Management Association willing to hold an area competition. Participants and local chapters should visit the Web site for more resources.
Awards/Benefits: The top prize is $10,000, and participants receive certificates of achievement.

American History Essay Contest

Contact: National Society Daughters of the American Revolution; 1776 D St., NW; Washington, DC 20006-5303. Phone: 202-628-1776.
Web Site: http://www.dar.org
Description: Entrants submit an original essay that addresses the topical focus for the year. Essays are judged on the basis of accuracy, focus on the topic, organization, interest, originality, spelling, grammar, punctuation, and neatness. Each chapter selects an essay at each

grade level to submit to the state competition. The state selects one essay at each grade level to submit to the regional competition. Each region selects one essay at each grade level to submit to the national competition.

How to Participate: Submit an essay in accordance with the guidelines

Cost: None

Categories/Content Areas: History and Language Arts

Ages/Grade Levels: Grades 5–8

Status: Local, state, regional, and national

Time Commitment: Varies depending on the time necessary to write the essay

Resources Needed: None

Awards/Benefits: The chapter gives each participant a certificate of participation, and chapter winners are given bronze medals and certificates. State winners receive certificates and silver medals. National winners receive certificates, medals, and a monetary award.

American Invitational Mathematics Exam

Contact: American Mathematics Competitions, University of Nebraska, Lincoln, NE 68588-0658. Phone: 800-527-3690. Fax: 402-472-6087. E-mail: amcinfo@unl.edu.

Web Site: http://www.math.unl.edu

Description: The American Invitational Mathematics Exam (AIME) is a three-hour, fifteen-question examination on precalculus mathematics.

How to Participate: Invitations are extended to all students in the United States and Canada who attain an announced cutoff score on the American Mathematics Contest 10 or American Mathematics Contest 12.

Cost: None

Categories/Content Areas: Precalculus Mathematics

Ages/Grade Levels: Secondary school students

Status: United States and Canada

Time Commitment: The exam takes three hours. Preparation time varies. The exam is offered three weeks after the American High School Mathematics Examination, which is held on a Tuesday in January or February.

Resources Needed: An invitation to participate

Awards/Benefits: The students who score highest on the AIME are publicized in the American High School Mathematics Examination Summary of Results and Awards. Each participant in the AIME receives a certificate of participation.

American Mathematics Competitions

Contact: American Mathematics Competitions, University of Nebraska, Lincoln, NE 68588-0658. Phone: 800-527-3690. Fax: 402-472-6087. E-mail: amcinfo@unl.edu.

Web Site: http://www.unl.edu

Description: The American Mathematics Competitions (AMC), formerly the American High School Mathematics Examination, is a series of national mathematics contests designed to challenge students' mathematical abilities and to identify students with exceptional mathematical ability. All tests are timed and in multiple-choice format problems that can be solved by precalculus methods. These competitions encourage students to "Make Mathematical History." Five competitions are offered: (1) the American Mathematics Contest 8 (AMC 8; for students in Grades 6–8 or advanced fourth- and fifth-grade students), (2) the American Mathematics Contest 10 (AMC 10; for secondary students), (3) the American Mathematics Contest 12 (AMC 12; for secondary students), (4) the American Invitational Mathematics Examination (AIME), and (5) the United States of America Mathematical Olympiad (USAMO).There also is a summer program offered, and the final six contestants are chosen for an international mathematical Olympiad.

How to Participate: The registration deadline for AMC 8 is early November. The deadline for AMC 10 and AMC 12 is early January. The registration form for each examination is available on the Web site listed above.

Cost: Varies according to the competition and date of entry. Registration fees range from $33 to $60, and tests are sold in bundles of ten for $11. Schools should bear the cost of these fees. If a student advances, there may be additional administrative fees.

Categories/Content Areas: Noncalculus Mathematics

Ages/Grade Levels: Grades 4–12

Status: National. Six students who are selected from the summer program compete in an international Olympiad.

Time Commitment: The time allotted to take a test varies by examination. Specific examination dates are established by test, beginning in November. Registration deadlines are November for AMC 8 and February for AMC 10 and AMC 12. The AMC 8 test takes forty minutes, and the AMC 10 and 12 tests take seventy-five minutes. The AIME is a three-hour test, and the USAMO is a two-day, nine-hour examination.

Resources Needed: Registration form, school entry fee, and the corresponding test-taking time on date of the examination. Registration forms and examinations are required. Additional study materials, practice sets that include exam questions, examination books, T-shirts, and math club materials are available for purchase.

Awards/Benefits: The Edyth May Sliffe Award for Excellence in Teaching is given each year to twenty teachers whose teams score the highest. Students who score at least one hundred on the American High School Mathematics Examination are invited to take the AIME. The top-scoring U.S. AIME students (according to a weighted average) are invited to participate in the USAMO. Intramural awards are presented at the school level. A school-winner pin or medal is given to the student in each school with the highest score. A gold, silver, or bronze medal is awarded to students who achieve the highest score in the school for four, three, or two consecutive years, respectively. An honor roll pin is awarded to those students with scores of one hundred or above.

American Mathematics Contest 8

Contact: American Mathematics Competitions, University of Nebraska, Lincoln, NE 68588-0658. Phone: 800-527-3690. Fax: 402-472-6087. E-mail: walter@amc.unl.edu.

Web Site: http://www.math.unl.edu

Description: The American Mathematics Contest 8 (AMC 8), formerly the American Junior High School Mathematics Exam, is a twenty-five question examination that focuses on seventh- and eighth-grade mathematical concepts. Areas addressed include mathematics, the arithmetic of integers, fractions and decimals, percentage and proportion, number theory, informal geometry, perimeter, area, volume, probability and statistics, and logical reasoning. For more information, see the **American Mathematics Competitions** section.

How to Participate: Registration brochures are mailed in early September to all public and private schools with seventh and eighth grades. The registration deadline is in October. The examinations are centrally scored at the office of the executive director.

Cost: Fees for each school wishing to register for the AMC 8 are as follows:

    Registration and standard shipping (Jan. 1–Oct. 10): $33

    Registration and expedited shipping (Oct. 11–Nov. 1): $43

    Registration and overnight shipping (Nov 2–Nov. 10): $53

Categories/Content Areas: Mathematics
Ages/Grade Levels: Grade 8 and below
Status: National
Time Commitment: The examination takes forty minutes. Preparation time varies.

Resources Needed: Registration forms and examinations are required. Additional study materials may be purchased.

Awards/Benefits: Awards are given to all officially registered students who have a perfect score on the examination. In addition, a plaque is given to the top-scoring student in each state. Intramural awards are as follows: a certificate of distinction is given to student(s) who receive a perfect score; an AMC 8 winner pin is given to the student(s) in each school with the highest score; the top three students for each school section receive, respectively, a gold-, silver-, or bronze-colored certificate for outstanding achievement; other high-scoring students can purchase an achievement award pin and a certificate of merit; and one certificate of participation (which may be duplicated) is included in each school's examination package.

American Regions Mathematics League

Contact: Steven L. Adrian, Executive Director; American Regions Mathematics League; 506 Superior Rd.; Wilmington, NC 28412. Phone/Fax: 978-422-6675. E-mail: sladrian1@aol.com.

Web Site: http://www.arml.com

Description: The American Regions Mathematics League annual competition includes a team round, a power question, an individual round, and a relay round. During the team round, team members work cooperatively to solve ten questions in twenty minutes. The power question requires the use of mathematical analysis and proofs. The individual round allows participants to work independently on eight questions in a timed setting. For each of the two relay rounds, each team divides into five subteams of three members each; the answer to one subteam's question is used by another subteam to answer the next question.

How to Participate: Send the completed registration form and registration fee to: Linda Berman, American Regions Mathematics League Treasurer, 241 Central Park West, New York, NY 10024.

Cost: In addition to travel expenses associated with attending the meet, fees are $55 per student and a registration fee of $300 (early registration) or $350 (late registration). This covers all American Regions Mathematics League services, the student's overnight lodging, and two meals.

Categories/Content Areas: Mathematics

Ages/Grade Levels: High school

Status: United States and Canada

Time Commitment: Two days in June for the national competition plus other days for local and state competitions, as well as time needed to prepare. Contact the national office for names of those who have participated to ascertain time needs.

Resources Needed: None

Awards/Benefits: Participants receive a certificate of participation. At the conclusion of the competition, scores are tallied and prizes are awarded to high-scoring teams and individuals. An awards ceremony honors the winners.

American Scholastics Mathematics Competition

Web Site: http://www.asan.com

Description: This mathematics competition offers students an opportunity to compete with other high-ability mathematics students from around the United States.

How to Participate: Students' schools must be registered. Once the school is a participating school, six sealed examinations, to be administered on given dates each month, are sent. The highest achieving students' scores are sent to be ranked nationally.

Cost: Schools pay a $65 entry fee.

Categories/Content Areas: Mathematics

Ages/Grade Levels: Grades 7–12

Status: National

Time Commitment: Schools should register by July. Examinations take thirty-five minutes.

Resources Needed: A participating school, entry fee, and examinations. The Web site gives sample examination questions and specific examination dates. Schools may also purchase past examinations.

Awards/Benefits: High scorers receive an awards certificate.

American Society of Newspaper Editors, Quill and Scroll International Writing, Photo Contest

Web Site: http://www.uiowa.edu

Description: This program was designed to recognize individual achievement in journalism and scholastic publication.

How to Participate: Each school can submit four entries in each of the following twelve categories: editorial, editorial cartoon, news story, feature story, general columns, review columns, in-depth reporting (individual and team), sports story, advertisement, and photography (news-feature and sports).

Cost: $2 per entry up to $96

Categories/Content Areas: Language Arts/Journalism
Ages/Grade Levels: Currently enrolled high school students
Status: International
Time Commitment: Entries are due February 5 of each year.
Resources Needed: Official entry form, which can be found on the Web site listed above, and the entry fee. Visit the contest Web site for more categorical information and to view past winners' entries.
Awards/Benefits: Winners will receive the Quill and Scroll's National Award Gold Key. If winners are seniors, they may apply for a $500 scholarship.

American Veterans (AMVETS) Americanism Program

Web Site: http://www.amvets.org
Description: This patriotic program serves to teach kindergarten through twelfth-grade students about their American heritage, civics, and citizenship. Students design posters or flags or write essays, depending on their grade. Each year a different patriotic theme is introduced. Entries are judged on originality, composition, and adherence to guidelines.
How to Participate: Entry forms can be found on the Web site in PDF form. Entries are submitted to local AMVETS departments.
Cost: No entry fee. The minimal cost for participation materials varies.
Categories/Content Areas: Patriotism, Social Studies, History, Art
Ages/Grade Levels: Flag drawing is limited to Grades K–1, the poster contest is limited to Grades 2–5, and the essay contest is limited to Grades 6–12.
Status: National
Time Commitment: Varies. Entries are due at local AMVETS departments no later than 30 days before the national deadline of July 1.
Resources Needed: Entry form, art or writing supplies
Awards/Benefits: Participants receive a certificate of participation. First-, second-, and third-place winners receive U.S. Savings Bonds.

Ann Arlys Bowler Poetry Contest

Contact: Bowler Poetry Contest, READ Magazine, Weekly Reader, 200 First Stamford Pl., Stamford, CT 06912.
Web Site: http://www.weeklyreader.com
Description: In this contest, students submit their original poetry for review.
How to Participate: Attach a completed entry form to a poem and mail it by the deadline.

Cost: None
Categories/Content Areas: Poetry
Ages/Grade Levels: All school-age students
Status: National
Time Commitment: Varies depending on the time required to write a poem.
Resources Needed: None
Awards/Benefits: Winning poems are published in *READ* magazine; each winner receives a medal and $100.

ARTS Recognition and Talent Search

Contact: National Foundation for the Advancement of the Arts; 444 Brickell Ave., P-14; Miami, FL 33131. Phone: 800-970-ARTS (800-970-2787).
Web Site: http://www.artsawards.org
Description: This is a program designed to recognize outstanding performance in dance, music, theater, visual arts, photography, and writing. Each January, up to 150 outstanding performers are invited, on the basis of an audition or portfolio review, to meet in Miami for a program known as youngARTS Week. They participate in adjudications, auditions, classes, studio exercises, workshops, interviews, performances, and enrichment activities. A panel of judges in each discipline uses a two-step process to evaluate applicants. First, the panel reviews the materials submitted by the applicants and then selects candidates in each discipline for live adjudications.
How to Participate: High school seniors or, for candidates not enrolled in school, proof of age seventeen or eighteen years by December 1 may complete the ARTS application process. Depending on the discipline entered, applicants must submit audiotapes, videotapes, CDs, DVDs, films, slides, or manuscripts demonstrating accomplishment. Specific application procedures are provided.
Cost: A nonrefundable application fee is required: $30 per discipline category entered by the June deadline; $40 for each discipline category entered after the June deadline and before the October deadline. A small number of fee waivers (limited to one discipline or discipline category per eligible individual) are available for applicants who cannot afford the application fee. To apply, a past-year's tax return or other proof of income level is required. More information is supplied on the official application form. For those applicants invited to go to Miami, the National Foundation for the Advancement of the Arts pays for round-trip travel, lodging, and meals.
Categories/Content Areas: Dance (ballet, choreography, jazz, modern, tap, and world dance forms.)/Film & Video; a maximum of twenty finalists participate in ARTS Week./Jazz (keyboard, violin, viola, cello,

double bass, guitar, flute, oboe, clarinet, saxophone, trumpet, trombone, percussion, composition, and tuba); a maximum of five finalists participate in ARTS Week./Music (Keyboard [piano, organ, harpsichord, accordion], Strings [violin, viola, violoncello, contrabass, harp, classical guitar], Woodwinds [flute, oboe, clarinet, saxophone, bassoon, recorder], Brass [French horn, trumpet, trombone, euphonium, tuba]), Popular (piano), Percussion, and Music Composition; a maximum of two finalists participate in ARTS Week./Photography; a maximum of five finalists participate in ARTS Week./Theater (spoken only and spoken and musical); a maximum of twenty finalists participate in ARTS Week./Visual Arts (ceramics, costume design, drawing, graphic design, jewelry making, painting, prints, sculpture, textile and fiber design, theater and set design, and nontraditional and ethnic art forms); a maximum of twenty-five finalists participate in ARTS Week./Voice Classical (soprano, mezzo soprano, contralto, tenor, baritone, and bass; popular and jazz); a maximum of fifteen finalists participate in ARTS Week./Writing (poetry, short story, play or script, selection from a novel, and creative nonfiction); a maximum of twenty finalists participate in ARTS Week

Ages/Grade Levels: High school seniors (17 or 18 years old)

Status: National

Time Commitment:

June: Early postmark deadline for submission of application form and fee(s)

October: Regular postmark deadline for submission of application form and fee(s)

November: Postmark deadline for submission of application packets

Preparation time varies.

Resources Needed: Depending on the discipline entered, applicants must submit audiotapes, CDs, DVDs, videotapes, films, slides, or manuscripts demonstrating artistic accomplishment.

Awards/Benefits: Up to $300,000 in scholarships plus cash awards are presented to candidates who are judged as outstanding. An unlimited number of $100 Honorable Mention awards are granted to selected applicants who are not invited to Miami. Award categories are as follows: Gold Awards is $10,000 each; Silver Awards is $5,000 each; first level is $3,000 each; second level is $1,500 each; third level is $1,000 each; fourth level is $500 each; fifth level is $100 each. ARTS awardees are the only candidates eligible for consideration by the White House for appointment as Presidential Scholars in the Arts. Also, through the Scholarship List Service, the National Foundation for the Advancement of the Arts provides the authorized names of all ARTS applicants who are seniors in high school to colleges, universities, and professional institutions.

Association of Educational Publishers Student Publishing Awards

Contact: Association of Educational Publishers; Attn.: Weekly Reader "What's Your Story?" Student Publishing Awards; 510 Heron Dr., Ste. 201; Logan Township, NJ 08085.
Web Site: http://www.aepweb.org
Description: Weekly "What's Your Story?" competitions are held to honor the best in published nonfiction writing by students. The contest aims to inspire students to write compelling, true stories through good reporting and writing.
How to Participate: Participants submit three copies of their writing with the entry form and fee by the postmark deadline to the above address.
Cost: $45 fee per entry. Late entries must pay an additional $15.
Categories/Content Areas: Language Arts
Ages/Grade Levels: Grades 1–12
Status: National
Time Commitment: The entry period runs from October to March. Fees, entry forms, and submissions must be postmarked no later than mid-March. Check the Web site listed above for each year's specific deadline.
Resources Needed: Entry form, entry fee
Awards/Benefits: Three awards are given for overall student publications, and three awards are given for an individual piece of student nonfiction. Each winner receives a $500 check presented to his or her school, and a plaque. Teacher sponsors of winning publications receive a one-year subscription to a Weekly Reader publication.

Ayn Rand Essay Contest

Contact: Ayn Rand Institute, P.O. Box 57044, Irvine, CA 92619-7044.
Web Site: http://www.aynrand.org
Description: Students are invited to submit essays based on one of Ayn Rand's major works: *Anthem*, for ninth and tenth graders, or *The Fountainhead*, for eleventh and twelfth graders.
How to Participate: Participants should visit the Web site listed above and select their appropriate contest. Then, students choose among three essay topics. Students write original essays ranging from 600 to 1,200 words for *Anthem* and 800 to 1,600 words for *The Fountainhead*. Each essay should be submitted with a cover sheet by the deadline. Essays may be submitted via mail or online.
Cost: None

Categories/Content Areas: Language Arts
Ages/Grade Levels: Grades 9–12
Status: National
Time Commitment: Essays must be postmarked no later than March 30.
Resources Needed: Essay topic and cover sheet
Awards/Benefits: For the *Anthem* contest, prizes are awarded as follows:

> First prize: $2,000
>
> Second prize (5): $500
>
> Third prize (10): $200
>
> Finalists (45): $50
>
> Semifinalists (175): $30

The *Fountainhead* prizes are awarded as follows:

> First prize: $10,000
>
> Second prize (5): $2,000
>
> Third prize (10): $1,000
>
> Finalists (45): $100
>
> Semifinalists (175): $50

Baker's Plays High School Playwriting Contest

Contact: Baker's Plays, Attn: High School Playwriting Contest, P.O. Box 699222, Quincy, MA 02269-9222.
Web Site: http://www.bakersplays.com
Description: Single- and multiple-student authored plays on any topic are accepted. There are no restrictions on the number of plays an author or group of authors may submit. Although not required, it is recommended that the play have a public presentation prior to submission.
How to Participate: By the specified deadline, mail a typed and bound manuscript along with a statement from a high school drama or English teacher verifying that the author is a qualified student to the address listed above.
Cost: None
Categories/Content Areas: Drama
Ages/Grade Levels: High school
Status: National
Time Commitment: Varies by author

Resources Needed: None

Awards/Benefits: The author who is named the first-place winner receives $500 and a royalty-earning contract, and Baker's Plays publishes the play. The author whose play is selected as the second-place winner receives $250 and an honorable mention, and the author whose play is selected as the third-place winner receives $100 and an honorable mention.

BEST Robotics Competition

Web Site: http://www.bestinc.org

Description: This competition is a sports-like science- and engineering-based robotics competition. It was designed by BEST (Boosting Energy, Science, and Technology), a nonprofit volunteer organization, to encourage students to pursue careers in engineering, science, and technology.

How to Participate: Each school can have a team. Each team designs a radio-controlled machine that will be required to complete various tasks. Teams gather six weeks before the competition to receive identical kits of equipment, raw materials, and detailed rules.

Cost: None

Categories/Content Areas: Science/Technology/Engineering

Ages/Grade Levels: Middle and high school students

Status: National

Time Commitment: Varies based on the team, but is extensive: six to nine weeks; two to three hours per night; for one, two, or three nights a week, depending on the team

Resources Needed: Entry form, equipment kit, and mentor

Awards/Benefits: Some local clubs award scholarships

Biz Plan Competition

Contact: Independent Means, Inc.; 126 East Haley St., No. A-16; Santa Barbara, CA 93101. E-mail: mlittle@independentmeans.com.

Web Site: http://www.independentmeans.com

Description: This competition gives females the opportunity to start a business. Participants do not have to start a business; they only need to demonstrate a well-thought out vision and plan for a new business endeavor.

How to Participate: Participants submit no more than ten typed or handwritten pages with the entry cover page. Written submissions must follow the plan template provided on the Web site listed above.

Participants should visit the Web site for rules, examples, and contact information where they can address questions.

Cost: None

Categories/Content Areas: Business

Ages/Grade Levels: Girls ages 13–19 as of August 15

Status: National

Time Commitment: Plans are due in mid-November.

Resources Needed: Plan template, cover sheet, and three copies of the submitted material

Awards/Benefits: Three winners receive $1,000 cash, a Camp Start-Up Scholarship, and more.

Botball Robotics

Contact: KISS Institute; 1818 W. Lindsey, Bldg. D, Ste. 100; Norman, OK 73069.

Web Site: http://www.botball.org

Description: This competition has two divisions: (1) Botball and (2) Research and Design Website Challenge. In Botball, each team plans, constructs, and programs a team of robots and documents the process. The autonomous robots compete on a playing field without the guidance of remote controls. Coaches attend a workshop in which they learn about robotics, the game, and the tools and components for building a robot. They receive a kit that includes the materials to build two robots and are eligible for technical support during Botball season. In the Research and Design Website Challenge, participants research and post their findings regarding a robotics-related topic on a Botball Web site.

How to Participate: Submit registration materials and fee; coaches must attend a workshop

Cost: $2,300 registration fee

Categories/Content Areas: Science/Math/Technology

Ages/Grade Levels: Middle school and high school

Status: Local, regional, and national; there are thirteen regions

Time Commitment: The time needed to construct the robots and prepare the documentation varies. Workshops for coaches are conducted in January through March, and regional tournaments are conducted in February through May. The national conference is in July.

Resources Needed: A laptop computer that meets competition specifications and a Botball Robot kit

Awards/Benefits: A curriculum Web site and kit of tools and materials to build robots are provided. In each division, the first-, second-, and third-place winners receive trophies and grants that can be used to attend the National Conference on Educational Robotics or defray some of the cost of the Botball registration. The first-place winner receives $1,000, the second-place winner receives $500, and the third-place winner receives $250. Honorable mention winners receive two registrations for the national conference. Research and Design Website winners are accepted to present a paper at the national conference that is printed with the conference proceedings.

Canadian Open Mathematics Challenge

Web Site: http://www.cemc.uwaterloo.ca
Description: This contest is a qualifying round for the Canadian Mathematics Olympiad. It addresses Euclidian and analytic geometry, trigonometry, binomial theorem, and elementary number theory.
How to Participate: Students register, and in late November they complete a paper-and-pencil examination in two and one-half hours. The examination is divided into two parts with a total of twelve problems.
Cost: $12 entry fee
Categories/Content Areas: Mathematics
Ages/Grade Levels: Secondary students
Status: International
Time Commitment: Varies depending on students' preparation
Resources Needed: Students may visit the above Web site for preparation resources.
Awards/Benefits: Approximately fifty students will be invited to the Olympiad, which is held in March. The top-ranked student in each region may receive a plaque. A maximum of nine medals may be awarded, and the top 25% will receive a certificate of distinction. Names of the top-ranking students may be listed in the results book on the Centre for Education in Mathematics and Computing Web site. All awards are up to the discretion of the Canadian Open Mathematics Challenge committee.

CANE (Classical Association of New England) Writing Contest

Contact: St. Paul's School, 325 Pleasant St., Concord, NH 03301. Phone: 413-542-8126. E-mail: cdamon@amherst.edu.
Web Site: http://www.caneweb.org
Description: This is a regional writing contest for middle and high school students interested in the classics.
How to Participate: Students submit a short story, poem, drama, or essay on a classical subject. Projects should be no more than 700 words.
Cost: None
Categories/Content Areas: Language Arts

Ages/Grade Levels: Grades 7–12
Status: Regional. Students in New England may participate.
Time Commitment: The registration deadline is mid-December.
Resources Needed: A statement indicating that the work is your own. Guidelines for writing this statement can be found on this contest's Web site.
Awards/Benefits: Three top winners in each state will win certificates and prizes. The New Englandwide winner will receive a certificate and a U.S. Savings Bond.

Christopher Columbus Awards

Contact: Christopher Columbus Awards; 105 Terry Dr., Ste. 120; Newton, PA 18940. Phone: 800-291-6020. E-mail: success@edumedia.com.
Web Site: http://www.christophercolumbusawards.com
Description: This competition uses science and technology to allow students to gain hands-on experience with real-world problems using the scientific method.
How to Participate: With the help of an adult coach, students work in teams to identify a problem and use the scientific method to develop a solution, just as scientists do.
Cost: Varies. There is no entry fee.
Categories/Content Areas: Science/Technology/Problem Solving
Ages/Grade Levels: Grades 6–8
Status: National
Time Commitment: The entry deadline is mid-February. Finalists' teams will need to commit one week for the National Championship Week.
Resources Needed: Varies on the basis of issue and solution development. All teams need a coach and entry forms. Finalists' teams need a week of time.
Awards/Benefits: Every participating team receives a certificate and judges' feedback, thirty semifinalist teams win a T-shirt and certificate of participation, and eight finalist teams and their coaches receive and all-expense paid trip to Walt Disney World to attend National Championship Week as well as a $200 grant to further their ideas. Two gold-medal winning teams receive a plaque and a $2,000 U.S. Savings Bond for each team member and a plaque for their school. One team will receive a $25,000 grant to help bring its idea into reality.

Civic Education Project: Civic Week

Contact: Civic Education Project, 617 Dartmouth Pl., Evanston, IL 60208. Phone: 847-467-2572. E-mail: cep@northwestern.edu.

Web Site: http://www.ctd.northwestern.edu

Description: This project was designed to bring together diverse groups of extraordinary students for a weeklong service-learning experience in host communities throughout the United States. Students learn about social issues, contribute to efforts to positively affect needy communities and, while doing so, develop important skills.

How to Participate: Students in Grades 9–12 who have an interest in learning about social issues, communities, and active citizenship who can demonstrate a high level of academic ability can apply. Students must submit the materials listed in the **Resources Needed** section.

Cost: The $775 tuition fee covers all expenses. Some financial aid is available to those in need.

Categories/Content Areas: Current Events/Social Studies/Public Policy

Ages/Grade Levels: Grades 9–12

Status: National

Time Commitment: The registration deadline is mid-February. Civic Weeks occur throughout the spring in different locations.

Resources Needed: Tuition fee, application for admission, student essay, grade report, recommendation letter, $100 deposit

Awards/Benefits: Students can earn academic credit, meet new people, earn service hours, and experience college life.

Clarke–Bradbury Science Fiction Competition

Web Site: http://www.itsf.org

Description: This international competition is designed to encourage original ideas for future space technology. This contest links the space community with writers and encourages young people to become more involved in science and physics and to share their ideas with others. Participants complete a science fiction story and/or a creative piece of artwork. Each year has a different theme, and participants are asked to incorporate the theme into their work. Entries are judged on use of technology in the story, creativity and innovative ideas, storyline, plot, characters, clarity, style, realism, and convincing description.

How to Participate: Write a science fiction story and/or create a piece of artwork. Stories should not exceed 2,500 words. Artwork can be a drawing, painting, digital image, and so on. Participants are limited to one story and/or one piece of artwork. Stories must be written in English.

Cost: None

Categories/Content Areas: Science/Science Fiction/Art

Ages/Grade Levels: Open to all

Status: National
Time Commitment: Time for story development and artwork varies. Entries are due in February.
Resources Needed: The registration form, which can found at the Web site listed above. Entries should include the following information: full name, address, phone number, fax number, e-mail, date of birth, sex, and nationality.
Awards/Benefits: The winner in each category receives $600, and the runners-up in each category receive $300. Each winner also receives three European Space Agency publications, including the European Space Agency brochure on innovative technologies from science fiction.

Classical Association of New England

Contact: Ruth L. Breindel, President; Moses Brown School; 250 Lloyd Ave.; Providence, RI 02906. Phone: 401-831-7350.
Web Site: http://www.caneweb.org
Description: This is an essay competition related to the classics. The topic is assigned each year. The essay's word limit is 700.
How to Participate: Students enrolled in a classics course are eligible to enter. If a teacher is not a member of the Classical Association of New England, then the name of the state representative can be supplied by the association president. Send winning essays to the state representative. The contest guidelines are published in the association's journal.
Cost: None
Categories/Content Areas: Writing/Language Arts
Ages/Grade Levels: High school juniors and seniors
Status: Regional (five New England states)
Time Commitment: Varies by individual. The entry deadline is mid-December.
Resources Needed: Competition guidelines are published in the association's journal, *New England Classical Newsletter and Journal*
Awards/Benefits: A $200 U.S. Savings Bond is awarded for best essay and first place only.

Concord Review Emerson Prize

Contact: *The Concord Review*; 730 Boston Post Rd., Ste. 24; Sudbury, MA 01776. Phone: 800-331-5007 and 978-443-0022. E-mail: fitzhugh @tcr.org.
Web Site: http://www.tcr.org

Description: The Emerson Prize is a $3,000 award given to students who publish in *The Concord Review* and have shown academic progress in history.

How to Participate: High school students who wish to participate may submit essays on a historical topic to *The Concord Review*. These essays should be between 4,000 and 6,000 words in length. Essays are accepted on a rolling admission basis. *The Concord Review* is published quarterly. Once a student publishes an essay in this review, he or she will be considered for the Emerson Prize.

Cost: $40, to be paid on essay submission

Categories/Content Areas: History/Language Arts

Ages/Grade Levels: High school

Status: International

Time Commitment: Varies

Resources Needed: Entry fee and entry form, which can be found on the above Web site. Potential participants may also want to visit the Web site for rules and regulations, frequently asked questions, and sample essays.

Awards/Benefits: $3,000 prize

Continental Mathematics League

Contact: Joseph Quartararo, President; Continental Mathematics League; P.O. Box 5477; St. James, NY 11780-0605. Phone: 613-584-2016.

Web Site: http://www.continentalmathematicsleague.com

Description: The Continental Mathematics League (CML) offers activities for students in Grades 2–9, plus a calculus league for high school and a Java computer competition.

Grades 2–3: Activities to approach problem solving and supplement a school program.

Pythagorean and Euclidean Divisions, Grades 4–9: Participating students must have above-average reading comprehension and analytical reasoning capabilities. Their computational skills should be appropriate to their grade level.

Calculus League, Advanced Placement (AP): The questions are designed to enhance understanding of calculus. At the same time, they prepare students for the AB level of the AP examination. Calculators approved by the Educational Testing Service may be used.

Java Computer Contest: The questions are based on the AP Computer Science Outline and should provide an excellent review before the AP examination.

Students work independently on timed exercises using only paper and pencil to solve problems. Contest dates are established by the CML and proctored and graded by the school personnel using answer keys and step-by-step solutions provided by the CML. Two copies of the contest questions are provided and may be duplicated as needed. There is no restriction as to how many students may participate.

The top six scores on each sheet are the team's score. The score sheet is sent to CML, where the results are collated and sent to member schools.

How to Participate: Schools must complete an official registration form (available from the address given above) and return it, with the appropriate fee, to the CML by mid-October (dates vary each year). The prices outlined below are the school's total fees for the school year.

Cost:

Grades 2–3 pay $75 for each team.

The Euclidean Division pays $85 for first team and $70 for each additional team.

The Pythagorean Division pays $85 for each team.

The Calculus League pays $85 for each team.

Computer Contests pay $75 for each team.

Categories/Content Areas: Technology/Mathematics
Ages/Grade Levels: Grades 2–12
Status: National
Time Commitment: Activities may be completed during class time.
Resources Needed: Registration form, available from the above address.
Awards/Benefits: Each participating team receives five certificates and two medals. National and regional awards are distributed to duly recognize individual and team achievements.

Creative Writing Essay Contest

Contact: Modern Woodmen of America, 1701 1st Ave., Rock Island, IL 61201. Phone: 800-447-9811.
Web Site: http://www.modern-woodmen.org
Description: Each participant writes a 500-word essay on a specified topic. At the local school level there must be at least twelve participants. Essays are judged on creativity, grammar, punctuation, organization, vocabulary, subject-matter content, and overall effectiveness of the essay. The Modern Woodmen provide brochures for students,

awards and ribbons for winners and participants, and necessary materials and forms.

How to Participate: Submit an application to the Modern Woodmen of America at least thirty days prior to the contest.

Cost: None

Categories/Content Areas: English and Language Arts

Ages/Grade Levels: Grades 5–8

Status: Local schools

Time Commitment: Varies by individual

Resources Needed: All forms and materials are provided by the Modern Woodmen of America.

Awards/Benefits: All participants receive participation ribbons, and a trophy is awarded to the first-, second-, and third-place winner in each school.

Cricket League Contest

Contact: Cricket League, P.O. Box 300, Peru, IL 61354.

Web Site: http://www.cricketmag.com

Description: *Cricket* magazine holds story, drawing, poetry, and photography contests each month.

How to Participate: Entries must be on the theme detailed along with the contest rules on the Cricket League page of each month's *Cricket* magazine. The theme relates to a story or article in that issue. Although the magazine targets readers from nine to fourteen, there is no limit on who may enter.

Cost: None

Categories/Content Areas: Language Arts

Ages/Grade Levels: All

Status: National

Time Commitment: The time required to produce the story, poem, or artwork to submit

Resources Needed: A current issue of *Cricket* magazine

Awards/Benefits: Each entry receives a reply, regardless of whether it wins. Winning entries are published in *Cricket* three months later. Winners receive certificates suitable for framing and prizes such as books and writing or art supplies. Numerous honorable mention certificates are also awarded.

Destination Imagination

Contact: Destination Imagination, P.O. Box 547, Glassboro, NJ 08028. Phone: 856-881-1603. Fax: 856-881-3596. E-mail: askdi@dihq.org.

Web Site: http://www.destinationimagination.org

Description: This competition encourages participants to develop their creative and critical thinking skills, teamwork, time management, and their ability to problem-solve. Participants compete in teams of up to seven to create unique solutions to a Team Challenge. Solutions can be a one of or a blend of several disciplines: theatrical, structural, improvisational, scientific, or technical.

How to Participate: Teams of five to seven choose among five competitive Team Challenges: Challenge A: Technical/Mechanical, Challenge B: Theater Arts/Science, Challenge C: Theater Arts/Fine Arts, Challenge D: Theater Arts/Improvisation, and Challenge E: Structural & Architectural Design. Teams register for the competition and pay for their team packets online. Teams locate local affiliates online to register for regional tournaments.

Cost: Varies. Team packets cost anywhere from $25 to $225, depending on the number of teams and whether the team has domestic or international status.

Categories/Content Areas: Problem Solving

Ages/Grade Levels: All ages

Status: Local, state, national, international

Time Commitment: Teams work together for eight to twelve weeks. Materials are released on September 1. Most teams organize between October and January. Depending on the team's advancement through tournaments, a team may be competing through the global finals, which take place in May.

Resources Needed: Local affiliates, registration forms and fees, teams of five to seven, and eight to ten weeks of preparation and competition time

Awards/Benefits: Awards vary on the basis of region and advancement.

Discovery Channel Young Scientist Challenge

Web Site: http://school.discovery.com

Description: This competition promotes exploration in science and engineering. Students participate in local science fairs by submitting the original research materials required by these fairs. Students become semifinalists by nomination. From these semifinalists, forty finalists are chosen. The forty finalists are chosen from the same verbal and written presentations required at the local level. These finalists, who are flown to Washington, DC, for a week of challenges and presentations, participate in the Discovery Channel Young Scientist Challenge to determine the winners.

How to Participate: Participants submit science projects in one of the science and engineering fairs affiliated with science service. Then, 6,000 entrees are nominated by their local fair directors and go through a selection process to decide on forty participants for the finals of the Discovery Channel Young Scientist Challenge.

Cost: Varies

Categories/Content Areas: Science/Engineering/Technology

Ages/Grade Levels: Grades 5–8

Status: National

Time Commitment: Varies according to individual and on the basis of the stage of competition to which the participant advances. The final round requires one week of competition.

Resources Needed: A local or regional science fair. Entry forms can be found online at the Web site listed above.

Awards/Benefits: At the nominee stage, students receive lapel pins and certificates. Students who complete an entry booklet will receive a T-shirt. At the semifinalist stage, students receive a certificate of recognition and a small prize; teachers also receive a prize. At the finalist stage, in Washington, DC, students receive the following: an all-expense-paid trip to Washington, DC; a special Discovery Channel Young Scientist Challenge shirt; a $50 gift certificate valid at any Discovery Channel Store, Discovery Channel catalog, or at http://www.discoverystore.com (as well as at any The Nature Company store or The Nature Company catalog); a chance to appear on television; a plaque for the student's teacher; a plaque for the student's middle school; and the Discovery Channel Young Scientist Challenge medal. At the winner stage, students receive scholarships: first place wins a $20,000 scholarship, second place wins a $10,000 scholarship, third place wins a $5,000 scholarship, and fourth through fortieth places win a $500 scholarship.

Doors to Diplomacy

Web Site: http://www.globalschoolnet.org

Description: This educational contest is sponsored by the U.S. Department of State and offered to middle- and high school students. Participants around the world, working in small teams, create Web projects that address the importance of international affairs and diplomacy.

How to Participate: Teams of two to four students and up to two adult coaches are created. Teams conduct research on- and offline and then, using that information, create an educational Web project. Teams also create a narrative that includes the organization of the project, the challenges, and support from local content standards. They also are required to conduct peer review on four other projects.

Cost: None

Categories/Content Areas: International Affairs/Diplomacy/Social Studies

Ages/Grade Levels: Grades 6–12/ages 12–19
Status: International
Time Commitment: Research and project creation times vary. Registration begins in late October and runs through February.
Resources Needed: Internet access and one or two adults to serve as coaches
Awards/Benefits: Each member of the winning team wins a trip to Washington, DC; a private tour of the U.S. Department of State; meetings with key officials; participation in a special awards ceremony; and a $2,000 cash scholarship. The winning coaches' schools each receive $500 in cash.

DuPont Challenge Science Essay Awards Program

Contact: The DuPont Challenge; 2007 Science Essay Awards Competition; c/o General Learning Communications; 900 Skokie Blvd., Ste. 200; Northbrook, IL 60062. Phone: 847-205-3000.
Web Site: http://www.glcomm.com
Description: For this competition, participants, who are nominated by a teacher at their school, write an essay of 700 to 1,000 words. Essays must be in English and are judged on the basis of the science content as well as creativity, spelling, punctuation, and grammar.
How to Participate: To enter, complete the entry form, staple it to the essay, have both the student and the nominating teacher sign the form, place all documents in a 9-in. × 12-in. (23-cm × 30-cm) envelope, and submit them by first-class mail on or before the deadline.
Cost: None
Categories/Content Areas: Science/Language Arts
Ages/Grade Levels: Junior Division (Grades 7–9), Senior Division (Grades 10–12)
Status: Local, regional, state
Time Commitment: The required writing varies from entrant to entrant. Entry deadline is mid-February.
Resources Needed: Entry form
Awards/Benefits: In each division, the first-place winner receives $3,000 and an all-expense-paid trip to Kennedy Space Center and Disney World. Each winner's teacher receives $500 and an all-expense-paid trip to Kennedy Space Center and Disney World, plus an all-expense-paid trip to the National Science Teachers Association Conference. In each division there are four finalists, each of whom receives $1,000. The teacher of each finalist receives $250. The honorable mention winners in each division receive $100 each.

Duracell/NSTA Scholarship Competition

Contact: Duracell/NSTA (National Science Teachers Association) Scholarship Competition, NSTA, 1840 Wilson Blvd., Arlington, VA 22201-3000. Phone: 703-243-7100 and 703-312-9258. Fax: 703-243-7177.
Web Site: http://www.rpsec.usca.sc.edu
Description: Following contest specifications, each entrant must design and build a device that runs on batteries and performs a practical function. This can include, but is not limited to, devices that educate, entertain, or make life easier in some way. Each entry must be designed and built by a single entrant. Joint entries are not accepted. When requested to send the actual device for final judging, finalists are to send the device in accordance with detailed shipping instructions. Packaging, including boxes and insulating materials, is the responsibility of finalists. Criteria for judging are as follows: 35% creativity; 35% practicality of the device; 15% energy efficiency of the device; and 15% clarity of essay, including spelling and grammar. Duracell and the NSTA accept no responsibility for damage to devices or loss of devices during judging, shipping, or reshipping. Entry materials (essay, wiring diagram, and photographs) are not returned to the entrants. The devices submitted by the one hundred finalists may be retained by Duracell for up to eighteen months. The student inventor retains ownership and rights to the battery-powered device.
How to Participate: Submit all entry materials by the specified deadline (around January 21). Do not mail the actual device. When requested, competition finalists send their actual device for the final judging. Each entry must contain all of the following:

> *Essay:* A description of the device, not to exceed two pages in length, that is typed or computer printed in black, double spaced with 1-in. (2.5-cm) margins on standard 8.5-in. × 11-in. (22-cm × 28-cm) paper.

> *Wiring Diagram:* A drawing of the device's circuit diagram that includes the polarity of the batteries and uses standard symbols, submitted on standard 8.5-in. × 11-in. (22-cm × 28-cm) paper.

> *Photographs:* One or more photographs (slides are not acceptable) of the device that show it clearly and in full.

> *Official entry form:* Call the phone number listed above to request a brochure and entry form.

Cost: Postage and cost of materials
Categories/Content Areas: General Problem Solving, Science

Ages/Grade Levels: Grades 9–12
Status: National
Time Commitment: Varies per individual
Resources Needed: Duracell alkaline AAA, AA, C, D, 9-volt, and/or lantern-size batteries; official entry form; photographs of device
Awards/Benefits: One hundred student awards of U.S. Series EE Savings Bonds in the following amounts are awarded:

First place (1): $20,000

Second place (5): $10,000

Third place (10): $1,000

Fourth place (25): $500

Fifth place (59): $100

Winners, their parents, and teachers/sponsors attend the NSTA National Convention awards banquet held in the winners' honor. Teachers of the top six winners receive personal computers. Ten third-place teachers receive a $50 gift certificate for NSTA publications. Twenty-five fourth-place teachers receive a $25 gift certificate for NSTA publications. Fifty-nine fifth-place teachers receive a Duracell gift. The top finalists receive a personalized award certificate. All participants receive a gift and a certificate.

eCybermission

Contact: Phone: 866-GoCyber (866-462-9237). E-mail: missioncontrol @ecybermission.com
Web Site: http://www.ecybermission.com
Description: This is a Web-based contest designed for students to explore how science, math, and technology work in their world. The contest allows students to compete for regional and national awards while working to help solve problems in their communities by proposing answers.
How to Participate: Students must have a team consisting of three or four student members. All team members must register by the end of registration, which takes place in early January. The team must also have one advisor who is at least twenty-one years old. Teams then select one of four "Mission Challenges" (Sports & Recreation, Arts & Entertainment, Environment, Health & Safety). The team researches and conducts experiments to find a solution to a real problem in their community. Students then submit their work before the competition.
Cost: None

Categories/Content Areas: Science/Math/Technology
Ages/Grade Levels: Grades 6–9
Status: National
Time Commitment: Varies by team, but time commitment reflects the time students spend on other long-term projects. Registration is in January, and the deadline for submission of completed mission challenges is in February.
Resources Needed: Registration form, which can be found online at the Web site listed above, and computers with Internet access. Students cannot complete the competition without Internet and computer access. The team advisor must also have an e-mail account.
Awards/Benefits: Regional awards are given to the top two teams with the highest cumulative scores in each grade. First place receives a $3,000 U.S. Savings Bond for each student winner, a framed certificate, and travel costs to the National Judging and Educational Event. Second place receives a $3,000 U.S. Savings Bond for each student winner and a framed certificate.

In addition, four teams per region, per grade, win a $2,000 U.S. Savings Bond and a framed certificate in each student winner based on the highest individual score in each of the judging criteria.

Winning advisors receive a Materials World Module kit, which provides valuable information for classroom activities to enhance science, math, and technology skills.

National awards include a $5,000 U.S. Savings Bond, plaque, and medal for each student winner in the top team in each grade. All other national finalists (three teams per grade) receive a $3,000 U.S. Savings Bond and medal for each student winner.

Edventures Robotics Contest

Web Site: http://www.edventures.com
Description: This engineering challenge program was designed to promote enthusiasm in students by providing problem-solving scenarios and real-world teamwork experience. Various challenges are offered four times per year. Teams participate online.
How to Participate: Challenges are posted quarterly. Teams register on the Web site.
Cost: Varies
Categories/Content Areas: Engineering/Science/Technology
Ages/Grade Levels: Grades 3–12
Status: National
Time Commitment: Varies
Resources Needed: Computers, Internet access, Edventures Robotics Challenge Packs (available online at the Web site given above). No travel is required.

Awards/Benefits: Prizes are awarded for the following challenges: Best Solution to the Challenge, Most Creative Use of Materials, Oddball Award, Team Congeniality, and Most Autonomous Solution.

EngineerGirl Essay Contest

Contact: Grand Challenges Essay Contest; National Academy of Engineering; 500 Fifth St., NW, Rm. 1047; Washington, DC 20001. E-mail: webcontest@nae.edu.
Web Site: http://www.engineergirl.org
Description: This essay contest challenges students to think about the future and how engineering can meet the needs of the future.
How to Participate: Boys and girls can compete in teams of up to six to write a 500- to 750-word essay describing the challenge they believe will lead to the most important breakthrough of the twenty-first century. Students submit their essays with a cover letter by e-mail or by mailing a disk to the address listed above.
Cost: None
Categories/Content Areas: Engineering/Language Arts
Ages/Grade Levels: Grades 6–12
Status: National
Time Commitment: Entries must be received by May 15. Winners are announced in July.
Resources Needed: Students submit their essays and a cover sheet. Students can visit the Web site listed above to see previous winners' essays.
Awards/Benefits: First-place winners receive $200 and will have their essays posted on the Web site. Second-place winners receive $100, and third-place winners receive $50.

Federal Reserve Bank Fed Challenge

Contact: Deb Bloomberg. Phone: 617-973-3371.
Web Site: http://www.federalreserveeducation.org
Description: In this contest, students in teams of five analyze economic conditions and recommend monetary policy during a timed presentation before a panel of judges. Judges, who are Federal Reserve Bank economists and officers, question each team about their presentation and their knowledge of macroeconomic theory. Knowledge of the Federal Reserve, monetary policy, current economic conditions, responses to questions, overall presentation, research and analysis quality, and teamwork are the basis for judging presentations. This competition encourages economic literacy and the development of research and analysis, decision making, argument formulation, and effective communication.

How to Participate: Check with the Federal Reserve Bank for the district of your residency to determine whether that institution participates in this competition. All high school students in a given Federal Reserve Bank district are eligible to be members of a team that enters the challenge.

Cost: None

Categories/Content Areas: Monetary Policy and Economic Conditions

Ages/Grade Levels: High school students

Status: Regional (Federal Reserve district) and national

Time Commitment: Preliminary competitions begin in April and conclude with the national competition in May. Preparation time varies by individual and team.

Resources Needed: There is no fee to participate. Participant information and materials are provided by participating Federal Reserve Banks. Team travel to the national competition is provided by the participating Federal Reserve Bank.

Awards/Benefits: One team per participating Federal Reserve district competes at the national competition in Washington, DC. Winners in each division receive U.S. Savings Bonds. Some regions offer an overall winner a paid summer internship at the Federal Reserve Bank. The winning essay is published in each bank's regional magazine. Winners and their teachers are invited to a workshop, luncheon, and awards program.

Federal Reserve Bank Student Essay Contest

Contact: Regional Federal Reserve Bank district offices in Cleveland, OH (http://www.clevelandfed.org/Education/); Dallas, TX (http://www.dallasfed.org/educate/); Minneapolis, MN (http://www.minneapolisfed.org/Education); Richmond, VA (http://www.richmondfed.org/Education/); and St. Louis, MO (http://www.stlouisfed.org/Education/)

Web Site: http://www.federalreserveeducation.org

Description: This essay contest requires the use of critical thinking, argumentative writing, and investigative research skills in the preparation of an essay that focuses on a topic that is different each year and that relates to current events and community issues. Essays are judged on understanding of the topic, organization, conclusions, creativity, and writing style. In addition to the development of writing and thinking skills, the contest informs participants about the Federal Reserve's role as a regulator of the banking industry.

How to Participate: Check with the Federal Reserve Bank for the district of your residency to determine whether that institution conducts this competition. All eleventh- and twelfth-grade high school students in a given Federal Reserve Bank district may enter the essay contest for that bank if the following three conditions are met:

1. Each entrant must be under the supervision and direction of a teacher.

2. The supervising teacher's verification of authenticity, confirming that the essay represents the student's own thoughts and writing, must accompany the essay.

3. Students who have family members employed by that Federal Reserve Bank or who serve as contest judges are not eligible to participate.

Application for resource packets does not obligate students to enter.

Cost: None
Categories/Content Areas: Current Events, Banking, and Community Issues; Writing; Grammar/Language Arts; Social Studies
Ages/Grade Levels: High school students
Status: Regional (Federal Reserve district)
Time Commitment: Writing time varies by individual. The schedule varies by region. The essay submission deadline is in the spring.
Resources Needed: Resource materials packets are sent to teachers, who send in the application form. Each packet includes contest rules, entry guidelines and timetable, background information on the essay topic, applicable Federal Reserve publications, glossary of terms, bibliography, tips on conducting research and interviews, guidelines on preparing the essay, student entry forms.
Awards/Benefits: Winners in each division receive U.S. Savings Bonds. Some regions offer an overall winner a paid summer internship at the Federal Reserve Bank. The winning essay is published in each bank's regional magazine. Winners and their teachers are invited to a workshop, luncheon, and awards program.

Fire Fighting Robot Contest

Contact: David Ahlgren, Professor of Engineering; Trinity College; Fire Fighting Robotics Contest; 300 Summit St.; Hartford, CT 06106. Phone: 860-297-2588. E-mail: david.ahlgren@trincoll.edu.
Web Site: http://www.trincoll.edu
Description: The annual Fire Fighting Robot contest challenge is to build a computer-controlled robot that moves through a model house, locates a fire (a lit candle), and extinguishes it. Contestants receive the house layout with the official rules. Robots must be less

than 1 ft (0.3 m) on a side and can be tethered to a personal computer or operated by a self-contained microprocessor.

How to Participate: There are no restrictions as to who can enter a robot. Entrants may be individuals or teams. Registration forms, along with the entry fee, must be postmarked by March 15. Forms and contest rules are available from the address listed above.

Cost: There is a fee, ranging from $50 to $100, to enter a robot. More than one robot can be entered by any individual or group, but each entry must be accompanied by the fee.

Categories/Content Areas: Science/Technology/Engineering

Ages/Grade Levels: There are three divisions: the Junior Division, for students in Grade 8 and below; the High School Division, for students in Grades 9 and above; and the Senior Division, for participants who are out of high school.

Status: International

Time Commitment: The contest is held at Trinity College in Hartford, Connecticut, in late April. Although the actual competition takes place on one day, it can be the culmination of months of work designing and building the robot.

Resources Needed: Official registration form and contest rules

Awards/Benefits: The winner in each division receives a prize. In the High School and Senior Divisions, there are separate prizes for the winners in each category.

First Middle-Grade Novel Contest

Contact: Delacorte Yearling Contest; Random House, Inc.; 1745 Broadway, Ninth Floor; New York, NY 10019.

Web Site: http://www.randomhouse.com

Description: This competition was designed for middle-grade students to encourage the writing of contemporary or historical fiction set in North America.

How to Participate: Participants submit manuscripts ranging from 96 to 160 typewritten pages in length to the address listed above. No more than two manuscripts may be submitted by any single entrant.

Cost: None

Categories/Content Areas: Language Arts

Ages/Grade Levels: Ages 9–12

Status: U.S. and Canadian individuals who have no previous publications

Time Commitment: Entries must be submitted after April 1 and no later than June 30.

Resources Needed: A brief plot history and cover page to be submitted with the manuscript

Awards/Benefits: The first-prize winner receives a book contract with Delacorte Press for both a hardcover and paperback edition, $1,500 in cash, and a $6,500 advance against royalties.

FIRST Robotics Competition

Contact: FIRST (For Inspiration and Recognition of Science and Technology), 200 Bedford St., Manchester, NH 03101. Phone: 800-871-8326. Fax: 603-666-3907.
Web Site: http://www.manufacturingiscool.com, http://www.usfirst.org
Description: This contest, sponsored by the Society of Manufacturing Engineers, pairs high school students with professional engineers to design and build remotely controlled robots and use the robots to compete against each other.
How to Participate: Competitors attend a kickoff where they receive a common kit of parts and game rules and regulations. Participants have six weeks to design and build their robot. In regional competitions, the effectiveness of the robot is measured.
Cost: $5,000 for the first time a team attends the event and $4,000 for each subsequent year of participation.
Categories/Content Areas: Engineering/Science/Technology
Ages/Grade Levels: High school
Status: International
Time Commitment: Participants are given six weeks to design and build their robots. Regional competitions are usually held in the spring.
Resources Needed: Kit of parts, rules and regulations, entry fee, and mentor
Awards/Benefits: Participants are eligible to receive over $7.5 million in scholarships from engineering and science universities in the United States.

First Step to Nobel Prize in Physics

Contact: Maria Ewa Gorzkowska, Secretary of the First Step, Institute of Physics, Polish Academy of Sciences, al. Lotników 32/46, (PL) 02-668 Warszawa.
Web Site: http://www.ifpan.edu.pl
Description: In this contest, high school students conduct their own research in physics and write a paper of twenty-five or fewer pages. There are no restrictions to the subject matter of the paper except that the papers must have a research character and must be directly related to physics.

How to Participate: Papers are submitted with the entry form to the address listed above. Essays must be in English.

Cost: None to enter. Winning essay writers will be invited for a month's stay at the Physics Institute in Poland. If students choose to attend, they are responsible for their own expenses.

Categories/Content Areas: Physics

Ages/Grade Levels: High school

Status: International

Time Commitment: Essays must be sent by March 31.

Resources Needed: Two copies of the essay should be submitted with the entry form, which can be found online at the Web site listed above.

Awards/Benefits: Winners will be invited to the Institute of Physics for a one-month research stay. Honorable mention awards are also given.

First Young Adult Novel

Contact: Delacorte Yearling Contest; Random House, Inc.; 1745 Broadway, Ninth Floor; New York, NY 10019.

Web Site: http://www.randomhouse.com

Description: Participants submit manuscripts of 100 to 224 typewritten pages on contemporary young adult fiction topics.

How to Participate: Submit manuscripts to the address listed above.

Cost: None

Categories/Content Areas: Language Arts

Ages/Grade Levels: Ages 12–18

Status: U.S. and Canadian individuals who have no previous publications

Time Commitment: Entries must be submitted after October 1 and no later than December 31.

Resources Needed: A brief plot history and cover page to be submitted with the manuscript

Awards/Benefits: The first-prize winner receives a book contract with Delacorte Press. This includes a hardcover and paperback edition, $1,500 in cash, and a $6,500 advance against royalties.

Foundations for Life National Essay Program & Contest

Contact: Foundations for Life; 9841 Airport Blvd., Ste. 300; Los Angeles, CA 90045. Phone: 800-711-2670. E-mail: foundationsforlife@jiethics.org.

Web Site: http://www.ffl-essays.org

Description: Each participant writes an essay related to one of the Foundations for Life maxims listed on the Web site given above. Essay length varies by grade level: Third through fifth graders write 500-word essays, and sixth through twelfth graders write 1,000-word essays.

How to Participate: Participants must register at the Foundations for Life Web site to receive a free kit and then submit an essay.

Cost: None

Categories/Content Areas: Language Arts

Ages/Grade Levels: Grades 3–12

Status: National

Time Commitment: Varies. The postmark deadline is mid-March.

Resources Needed: Foundations for Life kit and a national contest entry form. Essays by former winners are available to read on the Web site.

Awards/Benefits: Participants have opportunities to win national scholarship awards; recognition certificates in Summa Cum Laude, Magna Cum Laude, and Cum Laude categories; recognition of participation; enhancement of college applications and resumes; and potential media recognition for students and schools.

Frazier Institute Student Essay Contest

Contact: Student Programs, The Fraser Institute, 1770 Burrard St., Fourth Floor, Vancouver, British Columbia V6J 3G7, Canada. E-mail: student@fraserinstitute.ca.

Web Site: http://www.fraserinstitute.ca

Description: In this contest, students analyze global issues and public policy and write a typed essay of 1,000 to 1,500 words.

How to Participate: Participants submit a cover sheet with their personal information and an essay written in English or French with references. Entries may be e-mailed as an attachment to the above e-mail address with the subject header "Essay contest entry," or they can be mailed to the address listed above.

Cost: None

Categories/Content Areas: Language Arts/Public Policy

Ages/Grade Levels: High school to graduate students. Students only.

Status: International

Time Commitment: The submission deadline is June 1.

Resources Needed: Cover sheet and recommendation letters. Participants may also want to visit the Web site for each year's theme and further entry information.

Awards/Benefits: $1,750 in cash prizes is awarded. First prize is $1,000, second prize is $500, High School category is $250.

Freedoms Foundation National Awards Program

Web site: http://www.freedomsfoundation.com
Description: This program recognizes contributions made by individuals, organizations, corporations, and schools to communities and the United States through citizenship.
How to Participate: Nominated participants submit one scrapbook or one book of photos, news clippings, and letters of recommendation, along with a one-page summary of why they should be chosen.
Cost: None
Categories/Content Areas: Human Rights/Freedom/Language Arts
Ages/Grade Levels: Grades K–12
Status: National
Time Commitment: Varies. The entry deadline is in June.
Resources Needed: Three-ring binder and materials for book, a one-page summary, and a nomination
Awards/Benefits: The first-place winner in the Youth category receives a $100 U.S. Savings Bond and a George Washington Honor Medal. The winner of the Military category wins a $50 U.S. Savings Bond. Other recipients receive a George Washington Honor Medal.

Future City Competition

Contact: Phone: 877-636-9578. E-mail: info@futurecity.org.
Web Site: http://www.futurecity.org
Description: This competition uses hands-on engineering applications to present the participants' version of a future city.
How to Participate: Only one team from each registered school can compete. Teams consist of three members, an engineer/mentor, and a teacher. Teams create a city using SimCity software and build the design into a scale model. Each team must write an essay and present their design.
Cost: There is a $100 limit on materials bought to build the model. Students must attend a registered school. The school registration fee is $25.
Categories/Content Areas: Engineering/Math/Science
Ages/Grade Levels: Grades 7 and 8
Status: Regional and national
Time Commitment: Regional competitions are held around the country in January. Finals are held in February in Washington, DC.
Resources Needed: Teamwork, research and presentation skills, computer skills, practical math and science application, SimCity software, competition handbook, and entry forms.

Awards/Benefits: The top team from each region qualifies for the national competition in Washington, DC. Qualifying teams receive free airfare and hotel accommodations in Washington, DC. The first-place team at the national competition wins a trip to the U.S. Space Camp. Prizes also include scholarships, computers, and U.S. Savings Bonds. Teams are also eligible for special awards sponsored by various organizations and engineering societies.

Future Problem Solving Program

Contact: Future Problem Solving Program International, 2015 Grant Pl., Melbourne, FL 32901. Phone: 800-256-1499. Fax: 321-768-0097. E-mail: mail@fpsp.org.
Web Site: http://www.fpsp.org
Description: This is a yearlong program in which teams of four students use a six-step process to solve problems. There are four categories:

Individual Problem Solving: Independent work of a single student.

Action-Based Problem Solving: A noncompetitive process for use in classrooms to introduce the skills of creative problem solving. Teams consisting of four to six students are encouraged to work on two topics, one per semester.

Community Problem Solving: A competitive process in which teams use future problem-solving skills to address a community, school, regional, state, or national problem. Teams work from hypothetical issues to real-world concerns. Teams that submit the best Community Problem Solving projects are invited to the Future Problem Solving Program international conference in June.

Scenario-Writing Contest: Students write a scenario of 1,500 words or fewer that is based on scenarios at least twenty years into the future.

How to Participate: Contact the office listed above for the names of state or territory contacts. The state office provides information on participation. Teams and individuals must have a coach. Participation must begin in a school. At intervals throughout the year, each team mails their work to evaluators, who return it with suggestions for improvement.
Cost: Varies from state to state. There is usually a cost per team or individual who enters.
Ages/Grade Levels: Primary (Grades K–3), Junior (Grades 4–6), Middle (Grades 7–9), and Senior (Grades 10–12)

Status: International
Time Commitment: The regular program is conducted over the course of the school year. Time commitment varies but usually decreases as students become more experienced.
Resources Needed: There are many materials available to help coaches. Of particular use is the *Coaches Handbook*. All are available at minimal cost from the state and international offices.
Awards/Benefits: Each state and territory has a state "bowl" competition in the spring. Finalists from this usually receive certificates and plaques. Some states award scholarships. State finalists proceed to the international bowl held in June. International competition winners receive certificates and plaques.

George S. & Stella M. Knight Essay Contest

Contact: National Society of the Sons of the American Revolution, 1000 S. Fourth St., Louisville, KY 40203. Phone: 740-695-4542. E-mail: Perkins6275@sbcglobal.net.
Web Site: http://www.sar.org
Description: This is an essay contest in which participants write about the events that shaped American history. The essays must deal with an event, person, philosophy, or ideal associated with the American Revolution, the Declaration of Independence, or the framing of the U.S. Constitution.
How to Participate: Contact local Sons of the American Revolution chairmen for specific submission information, and visit the Web site listed above for specific rules for writing an essay.
Cost: None
Categories/Content Areas: Language Arts/Social Studies/History
Ages/Grade Levels: Grades 9–12
Status: Local, state, national
Time Commitment: Varies. The submission deadline is December 31.
Resources Needed: Title page, essay, bibliography, and contestant biography
Awards/Benefits: State and chapter awards vary. Students can contact their local chairmen for specific information. National awards are as follows: first place wins $2,500, a certificate and medal, and airfare and hotel for two at the annual congress in Virginia. Second place receives $1,000, and third place receives $500. The winning essay will also be submitted for publication in *The SAR Magazine*.

Harry Singer Foundation Essay Contests

Contact: Harry Singer Foundation, P.O. Box 223159, Carmel, CA 93922. E-mail: director@singerfoundation.org.

Web Site: http://www.singerfoundation.org
Description: Participants submit an essay of 750 to 1,000 words that reports their research on one of the following topics: Alternative Fuels, Sunset Legislation, You and Your Community, What Does It Mean to Be American, and Enumerated Powers vs. a Living Constitution. Submissions are considered in one of three categories: (1) schools submitting ten or more essays, (2) schools with fewer than ten students submitting essays, and (3) individuals.
How to Participate: Send an essay via e-mail to staff@singerfoundation .org.
Cost: None
Categories/Content Areas: English/Language Arts, World Affairs
Ages/Grade Levels: Teens and older
Status: National
Time Commitment: Varies depending on the time the participant takes to conduct the necessary research and write the essay.
Resources Needed: None
Awards/Benefits: Each participant receives a certificate, and his or her essay is published online. The first-, second-, and third-place winners in each category receive $200, $100, and $75, respectively.

Harvard–MIT Mathematics Tournament

Web Site: http://web.mit.edu
Description: This is an annual math tournament.
How to Participate: Teams must first create an account and edit their roster. Teams then register for the tournament. Registered teams then compete in Boston in February.
Cost: There is a $10 entry fee per student. Teams must bear the cost of transportation to and accommodations at the tournament.
Categories/Content Areas: Mathematics
Ages/Grade Levels: Grades 9–12
Status: National
Time Commitment: Registration for the tournament is in December. The tournament takes place in February.
Resources Needed: Teams should visit the Web site listed above for information on registration, degree of difficulty, detailed schedules, past contests, and rules and regulations.
Awards/Benefits: Prizes vary.

High School Communications Competition

Contact: National Federation of Press Women, 1105 Main St., Box 99, Blue Springs, MO 64013. Phone: 816-229-1666.

Web Site: http://nfpw.org

Description: This contest recognizes excellence in the areas of communication and journalism. Twelve categories are judged: (1) Editorial, (2) Opinion, (3) News, (4) Feature, (5) Sports, (6) Column, (7) Feature Photo, (8) Sports Photo, (9) Cartooning, (10) Reviews, (11) Graphics, and (12) Single-Page Layout.

How to Participate: Students must first have received a first-place award in a contest sponsored by one of the federation's state affiliates (information can be obtained from the national organization at the address listed above). First-place state winners advance to the national competition. Students living in a state with no National Federation of Press Women affiliate may compete on an at-large basis. There are two At-Large groupings: (1) Eastern (Maine, Massachusetts, Maryland, New Hampshire, New York, and Rhode Island) and (2) Western (Hawaii, Oklahoma, Minnesota, Montana, Utah, and Washington).

Entries must be the work of the current school year, or the last semester of the senior year for student work published after the current deadline. Follow the deadline set by the National Federation of Press Women state affiliate. Submit two tear sheets (the entire page on which the article appears) for each entry. For photography categories, send two 8-in. × 10-in. (20.3-cm × 2.5-cm) or smaller prints plus the two tear sheets. Do not send photocopies, because entries are judged on the quality of the photo print.

Cost: Postage, materials preparation

Categories/Content Areas: Communications/Journalism

Ages/Grade Levels: Grades 9–12

Status: National

Time Commitment: Varies

Resources Needed: Entry materials

Awards/Benefits: First-place winners receive $100 cash; second- and third-place winners receive a plaque; honorable mention winners receive a certificate. Honors are presented during the High School Communications Competition Luncheon at the annual conference. National winners are invited to make remarks at the luncheon. Some state affiliates provide financial assistance to winners who attend the conference.

"Idea of America" Essay Contest

Contact: National Endowment for the Humanities; 1100 Pennsylvania Avenue, NW; Washington, DC 20506. Phone: 800-NEH-1121 (800-634-1121). E-mail: ideaofamerica@neh.gov.

Web Site: http://www.neh.gov

Description: This essay contest was designed to encourage students to think about the principles that unite the citizens of the United States. Each year's theme is posted on the Web site.

How to Participate: Participants register online and receive a user account. Participants submit one essay of 10,000 words or fewer online or by mail by the submission deadline.

Cost: None

Categories/Content Areas: Language Arts/Patriotism

Ages/Grade Levels: Grade 11 or students 16–18 years old

Status: National

Time Commitment: Varies. Completion of the online application takes approximately one hour.

Resources Needed: User account, cover sheet, application

Awards/Benefits: Each winner receives a $1,000 prize and will attend a national awards ceremony held at the Supreme Court. One grand prize winner will be selected and receive $5,000.

Intel International Science and Engineering Fair

Contact: Science Service; 1719 N Street, NW; Washington, DC 20036. Phone: 202-785-2255. Fax: 202-785-1243.

Web Site: http://www.sciserv.org

Description: The Intel International Science and Engineering Fair (Intel ISEF) encourages junior and senior high school students to use technology tools and science to explore. Attention is given to the quality of the participant's work and the degree of understanding of the project and area of study that is demonstrated. Judges both review the projects and interview the students. The local, regional, state, and country fairs may not be organized around the same project categories as the Intel ISEF. The Intel ISEF categories are as follows: Animal Sciences, Behavioral and Social Sciences, Biochemistry, Cellular and Molecular Biology, Chemistry, Computer Science, Earth Science, Engineering—Materials and Bioengineering, Engineering—Electrical and Mechanical, Energy and Transportation, Environmental Analysis, Environmental Management, Mathematical Sciences, Medicine and Health Sciences, Microbiology, Physics and Astronomy, and Plant Sciences. For both individual and team projects, the evaluation criteria include creative ability, scientific thought, engineering goals, thoroughness, skill, clarity, and teamwork.

How to Participate: From affiliated regional science fairs, two finalists are selected to go to the Intel ISEF. At the Intel ISEF, judges from the fields of science, mathematics, and engineering interview each student and analyze research projects using criteria established by Science Service. Science Service provides the official rules, a student handbook, and specific judging criteria.

Cost: The cost of materials for the project will vary depending on the nature of the project. The regional fair covers the finalists' costs for entry, transportation, meals, and housing.
Categories/Content Areas: Science
Ages/Grade Levels: Grades 9–12
Status: Local, regional, national, and international
Time Commitment: The Intel ISEF is one week. However, affiliate competitions occur throughout the year. Before the competition, time must be devoted to the preparation for and participation in regional science fairs. The amount of time spent is up to the individual.
Resources Needed: Materials for the science project
Awards/Benefits: Individual and team awards include cash, scholarships, summer internships, scientific field trips, computers, and laboratory equipment. Each of the top three finalists receives a $50,000 Intel Young Scientist Scholarship; a trip to the Nobel Ceremonies in Stockholm, Sweden; and a high-performance computer. A high-performance computer and a cash award are given to each Grand Award recipient. Grand Awards are presented to students in first through fourth place in each category: $3,000, $1,500, $1,000, and $500, respectively. The Intel Best of Category award winners, the top-scoring participant in each category, receive a $5,000 scholarship and a high-performance computer; also, the individual's school and affiliated fairs receive $1,000.

Intel Science Talent Search

Contact: Science Service; 1719 N Street, NW; Washington, DC 20036. Phone: 202-785-2255. E-mail: sciedu@sciserv.org.
Web Site: http://www.sciserv.org
Description: The Intel Science Talent Search, formerly the Westinghouse Science Talent Search, requires students to conduct and prepare a research report of a research project in one of sixteen areas. Group projects are not accepted. The research report must include a title page, a section delineating the purpose of the project, a section explaining the methods and results of the project, and a section describing the implications of the research and the project's contribution to the field. The report is limited to twenty pages.
How to Participate: Participants must complete a research report and fill out an online entry form. In addition, participants must submit three letters of recommendation from teachers and advisors. The recommendation form can be found online at the Web site listed above. If students conduct any of their work in a laboratory, then they must also have a laboratory form filled out by a scientist. A high school transcript and form to be signed by the student's principal also are required. All of these forms must be submitted by the receipt date. (Note this is not a postmark date.)

Cost: Materials for the research project, entry form

Categories/Content Areas: There are sixteen categories: (1) Behavioral and Social Sciences, (2) Biochemistry, (3) Bioinformatics and Genomics, (4) Botany, (5) Chemistry, (6) Computer Science, (7) Earth and Planetary Science, (8) Engineering, (9) Environmental Science, (10) Mathematics, (11) Medicine and Health, (12) Microbiology, (13) Materials Science, (14) Physics, (15) Space Science, and (16) Zoology.

Ages/Grade Levels: High school seniors

Status: United States and territories as well as American students studying abroad

Time Commitment: Entry materials are available on request beginning in mid-August. The deadline for entries is December 1. The 300 semifinalists are announced in mid-January, and the forty finalists are announced near the end of that month. The five-day trip to Washington, DC, for an exhibition of projects, selection of top scholarship winners, and awards ceremony, takes place in early March.

Resources Needed: Entry form, which can be found online at the Web site listed above; research report; three letters of recommendation from advisors or teachers (forms can be found online); and laboratory research form, to be filled out by the scientist whose laboratory was used

Awards/Benefits: Three hundred semifinalists each receive by mail a $1,000 scholarship. The top forty finalists receive a notebook computer; a five-day all-expenses-paid trip to Washington, DC, to participate in the Science Talent Institute; and a scholarship as follows:

First place: $100,000 (4-year) scholarship

Second place: $75,000 (4-year) scholarship

Third place: $50,000 (4-year) scholarship

Fourth, fifth, and sixth places: $25,000 (4-year) scholarship.

Seventh, eighth, ninth, and tenth places: $20,000 (4-year) scholarship

Thirty finalists: $5,000 scholarship

International Brain Bee

Contact: Society for Neuroscience, University of Maryland School of Dentistry, 666 W. Baltimore St., Baltimore, MD 21201.

Web Site: http://web.sfn.org

Description: The International Brain Bee is a live question-and-answer competition that tests the neuroscience knowledge of high school students. Students are questioned on topics such as intelligence, memory, emotions, sensations, stress, movement, aging, sleep, addiction, Alzheimer's disease, and stroke.

How to Participate: Students qualify for the International Brain Bee by competing in and winning local competitions. To register for local contests, students should visit the "Local Brain Bees" link on the Web site listed above.

Cost: Varies

Categories/Content Areas: Science

Ages/Grade Levels: Grades 9–12

Status: North America

Time Commitment: Dates for local competitions vary, but the national competition is held at the University of Maryland in March.

Resources Needed: Local contests are listed on the International Brain Bee Web site, which provides sample questions; information about local bees; registration details; and information on rules, regulations, and eligibility; as well as specific dates for the national competition.

Awards/Benefits: The first-place winner receives $3,000, an all-expenses-paid trip to the Society for Neuroscience annual meeting, and an individual trophy, as well as one for the student's high school. The winner also receives a fellowship to work in the laboratory of a neuroscientist during the summer. Prizes also are awarded for second and third places.

International Mathematics Olympiad

Contact: Walter Mientka, Executive Director; American Mathematics Competitions; 1740 Vine St.; University of Nebraska; Lincoln, NE 68588-0658. Phone: 800-527-3690. Fax: 402-472-6087. E-mail: walter@amc.unl.edu.

Web Site: http://www.imo.math.ca

Description: The International Mathematics Olympiad (IMO) is an international mathematics competition based on noncalculus mathematics. The IMO is held in July of each year in a designated country. There is also a USA Mathematical Olympiad (USAMO) and an elementary program.

How to Participate: The IMO is preceded by a four-week U.S. training program for twenty to twenty-four students. Selection for the U.S. training program is based on results of the American Mathematics Competitions, primarily the USAMO. Attendees are candidates for the IMO team. The IMO team is then selected on the basis of the USAMO and other tests given at the training program. USAMO winners are not guaranteed positions on the IMO team.

Cost: All expenses for attending the training program and travel to the IMO are paid by the Office of Naval Research, the Army Research

Office, and the Matilda R. Wilson Foundation. All expenses at the IMO are paid by the host country.

Categories/Content Areas: Noncalculus Mathematics

Ages/Grade Levels: Secondary school students who qualify, regardless of grade level

Status: International

Time Commitment: The training program lasts four weeks. The IMO takes nine hours, over two days.

Resources Needed: An invitation to participate

Awards/Benefits: If selected for the IMO team, students receive an all-expenses-paid trip to a foreign country and the opportunity to compete internationally.

International Student Media Festival

Contact: International Student Media Festival; c/o Association for Educational Communications and Technology; 1800 N. Stonelake Dr., Ste. 2; Bloomington, IN 47404. Phone: 877-677-2328.

Web Site: http://www.ismf.net

Description: This contest judges original media projects, animation, photography, video, and Web site design that enhance learning. Projects are judged on creativity, lighting, purpose, relevance, use of resources, technical quality, and overall effectiveness.

How to Participate: Mail a copy of the online entry form that is signed by the participant's sponsor (may be a parent, teacher, or other person 18 or older) along with the $20 entry fee and the media project.

Cost: $20 per participant

Categories/Content Areas: Language Arts, Math, Science, Social Studies

Ages/Grade Levels: Grades K–12

Status: Local, state, and national

Time Commitment: Projects may be submitted March through May.

Resources Needed: Media, $20 entry fee, sponsor

Awards/Benefits: Trophies and certificates are awarded to winners.

Invent America!

Contact: U.S. Patent Model Foundation, Invent America!, P.O. Box 26065, Alexandria, VA 22313. Phone: 703-942-7121. E-mail: inquires @intentamerica.org.

Web Site: http://www.inventamerica.com

Description: The Invent America! competition is conducted through local schools and families. Students go through the process of inventing—from brainstorming ideas, to designing a plan, to building and displaying the invention to solve an everyday problem. The enrollment kit contains lesson plans and activities for Grades K–8. Enrolled entities may submit one entry from each participating grade to the national competition. Criteria for judging student entries include creativity, usefulness, illustration, communication of ideas, and research performed.

How to Participate: Obtain a school enrollment kit from Invent America! The kit contains enrollment forms and other necessary materials. The school must return the completed enrollment form to Invent America! along with the enrollment fee. Entries are limited to one per grade per school, home school, or family.

Costs: $42

Categories/Content Areas: General Problem Solving

Ages/Grade Levels: Grades K–8

Status: National

Time Commitment: Students may spend considerable time developing their inventions. Classroom units are designed to be used during class time throughout the school year.

Resources Needed: Invent America! enrollment kit

Awards/Benefits: Awards of U.S. Savings Bonds are given for each grade in the following amounts: first place is $1,000, second place is $500, third place is $250, honorable mention is $100.

Invitational Mathematics Examination

Contact: American Mathematics Competitions, University of Nebraska, Lincoln, NE 68588-0658. Phone: 800-527-3690. Fax: 402-472-6087. E-mail: amcinfo@unl.edu.

Web Site: http://www.unl.edu

Description: The American Invitational Mathematics Exam (AIME) is one of the series of noncalculus examinations that comprise the American Mathematics Competition sponsored by the Mathematical Association of America. For complete information on this competition, see the **American Mathematics Competitions** section.

How to Participate: Students are invited to take this examination on the basis of their performance on the American Mathematics Contest 8 or the American Mathematics Contest 10. Top-performing students on the AIME are invited to participate in the U.S. Mathematical Olympiad. AIME results are centrally scored. The students encode their answers on answer forms, and these are sent to the American Mathematics Committee.

Cost: None

Categories/Content Areas: Noncalculus Mathematics

Ages/Grade Levels: Secondary school students

Status: United States and Canada

Time Commitment: The examination is composed of fifteen questions and has a time limit of three hours. Preparation time varies. The exam is offered three weeks after the American High School Mathematics Examination, which is held on a Tuesday in late February or early March.

Resources Needed: An invitation to participate

Awards/Benefits: See the **American Mathematics Competitions** section.

Jane Austen Society of North America Essay Contest

Contact: Marsha Huff; 777 E. Wisconsin Ave., Ste. 3600; Milwaukee, WI 53202. E-mail: janebrs@starband.net.

Web Site: http://www.jasna.org

Description: This essay contest was designed to foster interest in the life and works of Jane Austen.

How to Participate: Students complete the entry form found online and then submit six- to eight-page essays based on designated topics.

Cost: None

Categories/Content Areas: Language Arts

Ages/Grade Levels: High school, college, and postgraduate students

Status: International

Time Commitment: Essays must be postmarked before May 1.

Resources Needed: Entry form. Students should visit the Web site listed above for guidelines, topics, and judging criteria.

Awards/Benefits: Awards are given to each level: high school, college, postgraduate.

The first-place winner and his or her mentor receive a one-year membership in the Jane Austen Society of North America (JASNA), fees and lodging for JASNA's annual general meeting (AGM) or the cash equivalent, recognition at the AGM and on the JASNA Web site, publication of the winning essay both online and in the AGM booklet, and a Jane Austen novel of the winner's choice.

The second- and third-place winners and their mentors receive a one-year membership in JASNA, recognition at the AGM and on the JASNA Web site, and a Jane Austen novel of the winner's choice in the Chapman edition.

Japan Bowl

Contact: Japan-America Society of Washington; 1819 L Street, NW; 1 B Level; Washington, DC 20036.
Web Site: http://www.us-japan.org
Description: This competition is modeled on a quiz show format and tests participants' knowledge of Japanese culture, grammar, kanji, katakana, kotowaza, and onomatopoeic expressions.
How to Participate: Participants must complete and submit registration and agreement forms. Participants must be in teams of two or three.
Cost: None
Categories/Content Areas: Foreign Language
Ages/Grade Levels: High school students who are enrolled in their second, third, or fourth year of Japanese study.
Status: National
Time Commitment: Regional bowl dates vary. The national competition takes place in March.
Resources Needed: Eligibility form, agreement form, and at least two years of Japanese study. Participants may also want to download the competition guide from the Japan Bowl Web site listed above. They also will need to visit the Web site to find a regional competition in which to participate.
Awards/Benefits: Winners of the regional bowl are eligible to compete in the National Japan Bowl in Washington, DC. All regional participants receive lunch and a T-shirt. The first-place national winner receives a trip to Japan.

JFK Profiles in Courage Essay Contest

Contact: John F. Kennedy Library Foundation, Profiles in Courage Essay Contest, Columbia Point, Boston, MA 02125.
Web Site: http://www.jfkcontest.org
Description: In this competition, each participant submits an essay of 1,000 words or fewer about an elected official who demonstrated political courage as defined by John F. Kennedy in *Profiles in Courage*. The politician addressed in the essay cannot be John F. Kennedy, Robert F. Kennedy, or Edward M. Kennedy.
How to Participate: Complete a registration form and submit it along with the essay either electronically or by mail.
Cost: None
Categories/Content Areas: English/Language Arts and Political Science
Ages/Grade Levels: High school students under age 20
Status: Local, regional, state

Time Commitment: Essays may be submitted between September and January. The time required to develop an essay will vary.

Resources Needed: Participants can submit essays online or through the mail. Both require submission of an online registration form.

Awards/Benefits: The first-prize winner receives his or her award at the Profiles in Courage award ceremony in the John F. Kennedy Presidential Library and Museum. The event is hosted by Caroline Kennedy and Sen. Edward M. Kennedy. The first-place winner's teacher receives a John F. Kennedy Public Service Grant for $500.

Joseph S. Rumbaugh Historical Oration Contest

Contact: Chairman of the Rumbaugh Oration Contest, National Society of the Sons of the American Revolution, 1000 S. Fourth St., Louisville, KY 40203-3208.

Web Site: http://www.sar.org

Description: This oratorical event honors Joseph S. Rumbaugh, a Sons of the American Revolution member. The contest is designed to explore the influence of the Revolutionary War on present-day America. Contest entries consist of an original oration of not less than five minutes or more than six minutes. Topics deal with an event, a document within the context of the Revolutionary War, or a personality, showing the relationship it bears to America today. State societies and/or chapters of the Sons of the American Revolution sponsor preliminary rounds to select one winner from each participating state. In districts where no state society individually sponsors an entrant, a district entry is permitted. Before confirmation that a state or district winner may participate in the national contest, a copy of the speech and a photograph and a complete biographical sketch of the entrant must be received by the national oration committee chairman no fewer than fourteen days prior to the national congress. Judging criteria include composition, delivery, significance, history, and time. The delivered speech must be essentially the same as the script submitted, and notes may not be used.

How to Participate: Each state society makes contest information available to all high school speech teachers, history teachers, and principals as early as possible. Local contests are open to all students in all home, public, parochial, and private schools. Entry forms are sent to each state chairman on request, and general mailings to committee chairmen are made the third week in October. The national winner of the contest may not compete again.

Cost: Expenses for lodging, meals, and transportation to, at, and from the National Society of the Sons of the American Revolution congress may be paid by the sponsoring state society or district.

Categories/Content Areas: History, Revolutionary War/Social Studies, Speech
Ages/Grade Levels: High school students
Status: National
Time Commitment: Students should send a biographical sketch and other entry materials to the address listed above at least fourteen days before the contest. Individual speech preparation time varies.
Resources Needed: Entry blank, a winning seat in a local or district contest
Awards/Benefits: Scholarship awards are as follows: first place is $3,000, second place is $2,000, third place is $1,000. All other finalists receive $300, and all other national contest participants receive $200.

Junior Engineering Technical Society Tests of Engineering Aptitude, Mathematics, and Science

Contact: Cathy McGowan; Junior Engineering Technical Society, Inc.; 1420 King St., Ste. 405; Alexandria, VA 22314-2794.
Web Site: http://www.jets.org
Description: Tests of Engineering Aptitude, Mathematics, and Science (TEAMS) is an academic program and competition that helps students refine their academic abilities and build their problem-solving skills by working in groups. The one-day, two-part competition tests knowledge in an application, not just in a rote format that would be expected to be known by first-semester engineering students. Students work cooperatively in an open-book, open-discussion environment toward a single outcome on objective and subjective problems. In Part 1, the questions relate to engineering situations. In Part 2, teams solve more in-depth extensions to some of the problems posed in Part 1. Questions asked in Part 2 are more open ended and may require students to select one of several possible solutions and justify the selection. Demonstrations, tours, guest speaker presentations, and luncheons are available for participants to attend. One varsity team of four to eight students represents each competing high school. The team coach should be a high school faculty member in math or science. Coaches assist their teams in preparing for the TEAMS competition and make arrangements to participate. All Part 1 answers are scored on the day of the competition. Test scores for Part 1 equal the total number of correct answers. Competition hosts announce the local winners on competition day. State results are announced by the Junior Engineering Technical Society (JETS) national headquarters. On the basis of state rankings and the number of schools competing in each division, certain teams advance for national recognition.

Those schools' Part 2 solutions are forwarded by hosts to JETS national headquarters for evaluation and scoring by a panel of engineers.

How to Participate: Interested schools should submit the official entry form to JETS-TEAMS. Schools can either have their name forwarded to the TEAMS competition site in their area or take steps to establish their own school as a competition site. The national office has information on how to participate.

Cost: The registration fee is determined by the competition host. Participants can pay $35 for a set of former TEAMS examinations and answer keys to help prepare for the competition.

Categories/Content Areas: Biology, Chemistry, Physics, Technology, Mathematics

Ages/Grade Levels: Secondary school

Status: National

Time Commitment: TEAMS is a one-day event and is held between February and March. The amount of preparation time varies. Each part of the examination must be completed in one and one-half hours.

Resources Needed: A set of former TEAMS examinations and answer keys to help prepare for the competition

Awards/Benefits: TEAMS participants compete for local, state, and national awards. JETS national headquarters officially announces all state and national winners. JETS recognizes top-ranking schools at the state and national levels in each of the nine competition divisions. Locally, team awards are determined by the hosts. In the 1994 competition, among other prizes and awards, all team members of national champion varsity teams received a Hewlett-Packard HP32Sii calculator. Other awards are sought by JETS for national varsity and junior varsity participants.

Junior Science and Humanities Symposia

Contact: Doris Ellis Cousens, Director; National Junior Science and Humanities Symposia; Academy of Applied Science; 98 Washington St.; Concord, NH 03301. Phone: 603-228-4520. Fax: 603-228-4730.

Web Site: http://www.jshs.org

Description: In this program, students compete by presenting their original scientific research in science, engineering, or mathematics and discussing its impact on humanity. Forty-seven regional symposia are held annually on university campuses. Winners advance to the national competition, which is held annually in May.

How to Participate: The regional symposium director sends application forms to area schools, requesting nominations for symposium participants and paper presenters. Students submit an original research paper prepared according to the regional guidelines and the completed nomination form. A symposium review committee selects papers for presentation at the regional symposium and then, during the oral presentations, the finalists are selected for the national symposium. Five delegates from each regional symposium attend the national symposium, and one regional delegate competes with forty-six student researchers for international awards and scholarships. One student from each regional delegation is selected to present his or her research paper at the national forum, at the London International Youth Science Forum, and for scholarship awards.

Cost: None

Categories/Content Areas: Engineering/Mathematics/Science

Ages/Grade Levels: Secondary school, high school

Status: National (forty-eight contiguous states, Puerto Rico, and the Department of Defense Schools of Europe and the Pacific)

Time Commitment: The symposia are scheduled during the academic year. The national symposium lasts about four days. Preparation time varies by student.

Resources Needed: Application form

Awards/Benefits: Each year, the regional symposia present scholarship awards totaling $90,000, certificates of recognition, and other awards. The U.S. Army presents a $300 faculty award to the teacher and school of the top student researcher at each symposium. The U.S. Army supports an expense-paid trip to the National Junior Science and Humanities Symposia (JSHS) for five students selected from each of the forty-seven regional symposia. One student from each regional delegation is selected to present his or her paper at the National JSHS in competition for the London International Youth Science Forum, presented by the U.S. Army, and for scholarship awards contributed by the Academy of Applied Science. The U.S. Army also supports an expense-paid trip to the London International Youth Science Forum for winners of the National JSHS research paper competition.

Kids Are Authors

Web Site: http://teacher.scholastic.com

Description: This annual competition was designed to encourage the reading, writing, and artistic skills of children in Grades K–8 by creating their own books. In addition, children learn teamwork and cooperation by working in teams of three or more.

How to Participate: Under the guidance of a project coordinator, teams write and illustrate their own book. In picture book format, both text and artwork must be solely produced by the children. Teams can submit a fiction or nonfiction book from twenty-one to twenty-nine pages in length.

Cost: Supplies needed to create the book. There is no entry fee.
Categories/Content Areas: Language Arts/Art
Ages/Grade Levels: Grades K–8
Status: National
Time Commitment: Varies. Entries are due in mid-March.
Resources Needed: Art supplies and materials to make books; project coordinator; and entry form, which can be found online at the Web site listed above.
Awards/Benefits: One fiction and one nonfiction grand prize winner will have their book published and receive $5,000 in merchandise from the Scholastic Book Fairs to be awarded to the public/private school or nonprofit organization of their choice. Teams will also receive one hundred copies of their published book. Each winning student receives a medal and certificate. In addition, five honorable mention books are selected and receive $500 in merchandise to be given to the public/private school or nonprofit organization of their choice. These students also receive certificates.

KidsBookshelf Contests

Web Site: http://www.kidsbookshelf.com
Description: Two contests, one for poetry and one for short stories, are offered each month. Children can submit one entry per contest. Winners are selected on the basis of creativity, style, and originality.
How to Participate: Submit entries by the last day of each month using a form found on the Web site listed above.
Cost: None
Categories/Content Areas: Poetry/Composition/Language Arts
Ages/Grade Levels: 17 and under
Status: National
Time Commitment: Minimal
Resources Needed: Entry form, which can be found online
Awards/Benefits: $15 gift certificate for books

Kids Can Write Contest

Contact: Susan Katz, 535 Valley Park Rd., Phoenixville, PA 19460.
Web Site: http://www.netaxs.com
Description: This contest allows for individual and classroom submissions. Students or classrooms are able to submit a minimum of ten and a maximum of forty poems, which cannot rhyme.
How to Participate: Interested individuals or classrooms should complete poems that are between five and twenty lines in length and submit them to the contact listed above.

Cost: None
Categories/Content Areas: Poetry
Ages/Grade Levels: Grades K–1, Grades 2–3, Grades 4–5
Status: National
Time Commitment: Minimal. The postmark deadline is late April.
Resources Needed: Potential participants may want to look at the Web site listed above for sample poems, writing suggestions, and judging criteria.
Awards/Benefits: The winners will receive an inscribed copy of Susan Katz's poetry collection, *Looking for Jaguar and Other Rain Forest Poems*. Each student who enters as a member of a class is considered a contestant for the individual prize.

Kids Philosophy Slam

Contact: Kids Philosophy Slam, P.O. Box 406, Lanesboro, MN 55949.
Web Site: http://www.philosophyslam.org
Description: This program was designed to encourage interest in philosophy by students of all ages. It also promotes critical thinking skills and discussion with other students and adults. Children are asked to respond to questions such as "Compassion or violence: Which has a greater impact on society?" Depending on age, students submit an essay, artwork, poetry, or song.
How to Participate: Submit essay, artwork, poetry, or song, with a cover form, to the address listed above.
Cost: Schools must pay a $25 registration fee. For home-schooled participants, the cost is $2 per home school.
Categories/Content Areas: Language Arts/Poetry/Art/Philosophy
Ages/Grade Levels: Grades K–12
Status: National
Time Commitment: Varies. Entries are due in mid-February.
Resources Needed: Cover form and entry fee. Participants may want to visit the Web site listed above for more resources and contest rules.
Awards/Benefits: Each grade level has its own national winner. The top four high school students debate at the national finals. The winner earns the title of "Most Philosophical Student in America."

Knowledge Master Open

Contact: Academic Hallmarks, Inc.; P.O. Box 998; Durango, CO 81301.
Web Site: http://www.greatauk.com
Description: This competition, which occurs twice a year, allows students to participate in an academic competition without leaving

their schools. Participants can compete in teams with an unlimited number of members. Teams are given questions from a variety of curricula on a CD-ROM and compete from a computer in their school.

How to Participate: Participants print out and fill out the entry form found on the Knowledge Master Open (KMO) Web site, listed above. Participants send the form, along with a check for the applicable entry fee, to the KMO address listed above. Students may also purchase a practice CD.

Cost: The entry fee for spring/winter combined is $56. The winter KMO entry fee is $34. The spring entry fee is also $34. Students outside of the United States pay $74 for both competitions and $42 for one. The cost of the practice CD is $17 for U.S. students and $21 for those outside of the United States.

Categories/Content Areas: Academic Quiz Bowl (History/Mathematics/Language Arts, etc.)

Ages/Grade Levels: Grades 5–12

Status: International

Time Commitment: The event is held twice a year. Secondary students are given two and one-half hours to take the test. Fifth- and sixth-grade students are given one and one-half hours.

Resources Needed: Teams are made up of an unlimited number of students. Teams need entry forms and entry fee, a practice CD (optional), and computers to take the test. Paper and pencils can be used during the test.

Awards/Benefits: Division winners are given wooden plaques. In addition, the overall winners receive shirts. All teams receive participation certificates, posters, and stickers.

Laws of Life Essay Contest

Contact: Laws of Life Essay Contest; 5 Radnor Corporate Center, Ste. 100; Radnor, PA 19087. Phone: 800-245-1285 and 610-941-2828. E-mail: lawsoflife@templeton.org.

Web Site: http://www.lawsoflife.org

Description: This competition was designed to promote character education and encourages students to write about their values. It encourages writing and deep thought.

How to Participate: Participants are encouraged to write from the heart. Each community sponsors and organizes its own contest. Students should visit the Web site listed above for information about locating a contest in their area.

Cost: None

Categories/Content Areas: Language Arts

Ages/Grade Levels: Grades 3–12

Status: International
Time Commitment: Varies. Deadlines vary according to local contests.
Resources Needed: A local, community contest sponsor is required. Participants may also want to visit the competition Web site for sample essays and more contest information.
Awards/Benefits: Participants get an opportunity to consider the people and experiences that have shaped their values.

League of American Poets Free Poetry Contest

Web Site: http://www.poetryamerica.com
Description: This poetry contest was designed to find extraordinary poetic talent. It is open to all North American residents.
How to Participate: Submit one poem entry per person to the Web site listed above.
Cost: None
Categories/Content Areas: Poetry
Ages/Grade Levels: All
Status: National
Time Commitment: Minimal, but varies; there is no time limit on submitting entries.
Resources Needed: Internet access and entry form, which can be found online at the Web site listed above.
Awards/Benefits: Cash, prizes, and publication

Let's Get Real

Contact: Let's Get Real, 624 Waltonville Rd., Hummelstown, PA 17936.
Web Site: http://www.lgreal.org
Description: This competition gives students the opportunity to work on solutions to real business problems. Challenges may include environmental issues, manufacturing, distribution, engineering, software creation, human resources, health and safety, facilities design, public relations, or any other idea the involved corporations deem important.
How to Participate: Students compete in teams of two to six and choose a challenge from a list on which to work together to come up with creative solutions. Teams must first submit a registration form and a contract form and send these materials with their solutions. Forms are available on the organization's Web site. Finalists will be invited to an oral presentation.
Cost: There is no entry fee. Finalist teams that choose to attend the oral presentations must do so at their own expense.
Categories/Content Areas: Business/Problem Solving
Ages/Grade Levels: Grades 6–12

Status: National
Time Commitment: Deadlines vary. Check the Web site listed above for specific information.
Resources Needed: Registration form, contract form, a team of two to six students, an adult coordinator
Awards/Benefits: No monetary awards

Letters About Literature Competition

Contact: The Center for the Book; Library of Congress; 101 Independence Ave., SE; Washington, DC 20540-4920. Phone: 202-707-5221. Fax: 202-707-0269. E-mail: lettersaboutlit@epix.net.
Web Site: http://www.loc.gov
Description: In this competition, each participant writes a personal letter to an author in which the participant tells how the author's work has changed the way in which the participant thinks about him- or herself and the world. The author to whom the letter is written may be living or dead, and the author's work may be fiction or non-fiction, contemporary or classic.
How to Participate: Participants think about a book that inspired them and write a letter to the author to explain why. Participants follow the competition guidelines to submit a letter to the author of their choice.
Cost: None
Categories/Content Areas: Language Arts/Reading and Writing
Ages/Grade Levels: Level I is Grades 4–6, Level II is Grades 7 and 8, Level III is Grades 9–12
Status: State and national
Time Commitment: Varies by participant depending on the time required to research and write the letter. The submission deadline is in December.
Resources Needed: Each letter must be submitted with an entry form, which can be found online at the Web site listed above.
Awards/Benefits: Winners at both the state and national levels receive cash prizes.

Mandelbrot Competition

Contact: Greater Testing Concepts, The Mandelbrot Group, P.O. Box 20534, Stanford, CA 94309.
Web Site: http://www.mandelbrot.org
Description: The aim of this contest is to provide high school students of all ability levels with access to new topics in mathematics.
How to Participate: A mathematics faculty member at the school registers students online. The faculty member then receives the materials,

prepares the team for each round, proctors the tests, and forwards the information to Greater Testing Concepts.

Cost: The registration fee is $48 for both the regional and national competition. Teams registering for both competitions pay a fee of $72.

Categories/Content Areas: Mathematics

Ages/Grade Levels: Grades 9–12

Status: International. Registration fee must be paid with a U.S. check, and all testing materials are in English.

Time Commitment: Early registration begins in May. Tests are proctored by an administrator at any point during designated weeks. Test 1 is in October, Test 2 is in November, Test 3 is in January, and Test 4 is in March.

Resources Needed: Registration form; registration fee; and resources found on the Web site's "Resources" page, which includes welcome packets, links, and sample tests.

Awards/Benefits: Awards vary, but students who excel at the regional level receive ribbons.

Manningham Student Poetry Awards

Contact: National Federation of State Poetry Societies, Madelyn Eastlund, 310 S. Adams St., Beverly Hills, FL 34465. E-mail: verdure@ tampabay.rr.com

Web Site: http://www.nfsps.com

Description: The focus of this competition is the original poetry of participants. Each entrant may submit one poem to the state-level competition. Those who desire to participate but who live in a state that does not participate may submit an entry directly to the national competition. Only works that are totally original are considered. Poems that include portions that are another person's work are eliminated. Poems of fifty or fewer lines are appropriate. Each state submits ten poems per division to the national competition.

How to Participate: To enter, mail two copies of each poem—one without any identifying information on it and the other with the participant's name, school address, and grade on it—to the youth chair of the state. This information can be found on the Web site.

Cost: None

Categories/Content Areas: Poetry/English/Language Arts

Ages/Grade Levels: Junior Division is Grades 6–8, Senior Division is Grades 9–12

Status: State and national (Unites States)

Time Commitment: Varies by individual

Resources Needed: None

Awards/Benefits: The top ten poems in each division each receive a prize: first place is $75, second place is $50, third place is $40, fourth place is $35, five honorable mentions is $10.

MATHCOUNTS

Contact: MATHCOUNTS Foundation, 1420 King Street, Alexandria, VA 22314. Phone: 703-299-9006. Fax: 703-299-5009. E-mail: info@ mathcounts.org.

Web Site: http://www.mathcounts.org

Description: MATHCOUNTS is a competition in which individuals and teams solve problems in arithmetic, math logic, probability and statistics, linear algebra, and polynomials. The first level of the competition takes place at the school level. School personnel select both the team and individual members who advance to the next level. At all levels, the competition includes a Sprint Round, a Target Round, and a Team Round. The Countdown Round and Masters Round are a part of the national competition. Calculators may be used in some, but not all, rounds. The *MATHCOUNTS School Handbook* assists coaches.

How to Participate: By early December, participating schools must complete and submit the school registration form, which is available from the MATHCOUNTS Foundation. A school may send as many as eight participants: one team of four students and as many as four others who will compete as individuals. Students may participate in the coaching phase of the MATHCOUNTS program for an unlimited number of years. However, participation in the competition phase of the program is limited to a maximum of three years for each student.

Cost: $80 per team, $20 per individual competitor (limit of four per school)

Categories/Content Areas: Mathematics

Ages/Grade Levels: Grades 6–8

Status: There are four competition levels: (1) school, (2) chapter, (3) state, and (4) national.

Time Commitment: The school competition is in January, the chapter competition is in February, the state competition is in March, and the national competition is in May.

Resources Needed: Participating schools receive all essential materials. In addition to the *MATHCOUNTS School Handbook,* other coaching materials are available.

Awards/Benefits: At all levels of the competition, recognition and/or awards are given to winning individuals, teams, coaches, and schools. The top four individuals in each state-level competition receive an all-expenses-paid trip to the national competition.

Math Leagues

Contact: Mathematics Leagues, P.O. Box 17, Tenafly, NJ 07670-0017. Phone: 201-568-6328. Fax: 201-816-0125. E-mail: comments@math league.com.
Web Site: http://www.mathleague.com
Description: This competition evaluates participants' knowledge of a broad range of mathematical knowledge using a multiple-choice format. The fourth- and fifth-grade contests are administered at the school or district level, and score reports are not provided.
How to Participate: Order a contest kit
Cost: $30 per grade level for a set of thirty copies of the test kit for students in Grades 4–8 and Algebra 1; $75 for a set of thirty copies of the test kit for high school students.
Categories/Content Areas: Mathematics
Ages/Grade Levels: Grade 4 through high school
Status: Local and national
Time Commitment: Thirty minutes per test
Resources Needed: Test kit(s) are required; contest problem books and software are available for an additional fee.
Awards/Benefits: The highest scoring schools receive a plaque.

Math Olympiads for Elementary Schools

Contact: Math Olympiads, 2154 Bellmore Ave., Bellmore, NY 11710-5645. Phone: 866-781-2411.
Web Site: http://www.moems.org
Description: Math Olympiads for Elementary Schools is designed to afford teams of students the opportunity to participate in a national competition under the supervision of a local teacher without leaving their schools. The Olympiad is administered on a set date and scored at the school. Results are reported to the Olympiad. The Olympiad problems include the mathematical concepts of sequences, series, variation, divisibility properties for special numbers, magic squares, combinations, permutations, and cryptarithms. The team sponsor receives the prior year's problems and detailed solutions; each of the monthly contests with detailed solutions; and newsletters that detail procedures and important information.

There are two levels of competition: (1) Elementary (all team members must be at or below the sixth-grade level) and (2) Middle (teams that include members who are at the seventh- or eighth-grade level).
How to Participate: Schools interested in Olympiad membership must submit the registration form with the registration fee. A team is composed of up to thirty-five students. Schools can enter more than

one team. All participants must take the Olympiad simultaneously. The Olympiad competition materials are to be opened on the day of the competition.

Cost:

	Mail	Online
Teams in the United States, Mexico, and Canada	$99	$89
Teams elsewhere in the world	$150	$140

Categories/Content Areas: Mathematics
Ages/Grade Levels: Elementary and middle school (through Grade 8)
Status: National and international
Time Commitment: Five Olympiads are held at monthly intervals during the school year, November through March. Each Olympiad contains five problems, each with a time limit of two to five minutes.
Resources Needed: Registered teams receive all necessary contest materials. Additional materials are available for purchase.
Awards/Benefits: Participants who obtain a perfect score receive the Dr. George Lenchner Award, which is a bronze medal. The top scorer on each team receives an Outstanding Mathlete Award trophy. The top 10% of students in each division receive an Olympiad logo pin. The top 50% of participants in each division receive an Olympiad felt patch. Every participant receives a certificate of participation.

Medusa Mythology Exam

Contact: Medusa Mythology Exam, P.O. Box 1032, Gainesville, VA 20156.
Web Site: http://www.medusaexam.org
Description: This examination was developed to allow students who are talented in mythology to be recognized and excel. The Medusa Exam is a fifty-question test. Each year's examination has a theme, and participants should check the Web site listed above.
How to Participate: Participants download the registration form and mail it, with the entry fee, by the February deadline to the address listed above. The examination will be mailed to the participant's school and administered there.
Cost: $3 per student plus a $15 school fee. Financial aid is available if needed.
Categories/Content Areas: Mythology/Language Arts (Classics)
Ages/Grade Levels: Grades 9–12
Status: International

Time Commitment: The registration deadline is in February, and the test is administered in March. The alternate exam time takes place in April. The exam takes forty minutes.

Resources Needed: Registration form, entry fee, and exam materials, which will be mailed to the school.

Awards/Benefits: Top achievers receive medals that are imported from Italy. The highest scoring students are also eligible to apply for several achievement awards to aid in educational expenses.

Merlyn's Pen Literary Magazine Contest and Critique

Contact: *Merlyn's Pen* Contest and Critique, P.O. Box 910, East Greenwich, RI 02818. Phone: 401-885-5175.

Web Site: http://www.merlynspen.org

Description: This contest critiques the work of intermediate and high school literary magazines. The judges use a comprehensive checklist and a 500-point rating scale to evaluate each publication. Narrative comments are provided. In addition to overall awards, magazines may also be considered for Best Design, Best Writing, or Best Art and Photography awards.

How to Participate: School magazines must submit the following: two copies of the entry form; two copies of the same issue of the magazine; and a self-addressed, stamped envelope for returning the magazine and critique booklet.

Cost: Fees are as follows: standard critique is $60. Optional critiques: Best Design is $10, Best Art and Photography is $10, Best Writing is $15.

Categories/Content Areas: Language Arts

Ages/Grade Levels: Senior high or secondary school (Grades 9–12, 10–12, or 7–12), middle school or intermediate school (Grades 5–8, 6–8, 7–8, or 7–9)

Status: National

Time Commitment: Minimal, if the school has already produced a literary magazine

Resources Needed: Official entry form and a check or money order for the appropriate critique fee

Awards/Benefits: The best overall entry in each division, high school and middle school, receives the Golden Pen Award as well as recognition in *Merlyn's Pen*—with pictures of the magazine's staff, adviser, and selected pages from the magazine. Each of these schools also earns the Golden Pen Trophy. Merlyn's Silver Award (450–500 points) and Merlyn's Bronze Award (400–450 points) are also awarded to each magazine scoring within these ranges. These schools receive certificates of award. The winning schools in each of the special categories (Best Design, Best Art and Photography, and Best Writing) receive a plaque. All participating magazines receive a detailed critique.

Modern Woodmen of America School Speech

Contact: Modern Woodmen of America, 1701 1st Ave., Rock Island, IL 61201. Phone: 800-447-9811.
Web Site: http://www.modern-woodmen.org
Description: Each participant prepares and delivers a speech of three to five minutes that addresses a specific topic. Speeches are judged on subject-matter content; organization and logic; delivery style, including voice, pronunciation, enunciation, gestures, and poise; and overall effectiveness. At the local school level there must be at least twelve participants.
How to Participate: The school must submit an application to the Modern Woodmen of America.
Cost: None
Categories/Content Areas: Speech
Ages/Grade Levels: Grades 5–8 (recommended for this group), Grades 9–12 (described as beneficial for this group)
Status: Local school
Time Commitment: Varies by individual
Resources Needed: All forms and materials are provided by the Modern Woodmen of America.
Awards/Benefits: All participants receive participation ribbons, and a trophy goes to the first-, second-, and third-place winner in each school.

NAACP ACT-SO

Web Site: http://www.naacp.org
Description: ACT-SO is a major youth initiative of the National Association for the Advancement of Colored People (NAACP). Founded in 1978 by renowned author and journalist Vernon Jarrett, ACT-SO provides a forum through which African American youth can demonstrate academic, artistic, and scientific prowess and expertise, thereby gaining the same recognition often reserved only for entertainers and athletes.

ACT-SO is a yearlong enrichment program designed to recruit, stimulate, improve, and encourage high academic and cultural achievement among African American high school students. The ACT-SO program centers on the dedication and commitment of community volunteers and business leaders who serve as mentors and coaches to promote academic and artistic excellence among African American students. There are twenty-five categories of competition in the sciences, humanities, performing, and visual arts.

Cost: Not specified

Categories/Content Areas: There are twenty-five different categories, including Physics, Computer Science, Drawing, Playwriting, Dance, Sculpture, and Filmmaking.

Ages/Grade Levels: Secondary school

Status: Local; gold medal winners advance to national competition.

Time Commitment: Six months of once-weekly meetings on Saturday.

Resources Needed: A local program

Awards/Benefits: Gold, silver, and bronze medals are awarded.

NASA Space Settlement Contest

Contact: Bryan Yager, MS 236-7, NASA (National Aeronautics and Space Administration) Ames Research Center, Moffett Field, CA 94035.

Web Site: http://www.nsta.org

Description: Participants submit space settlement designs and related materials. Teachers are encouraged to use this contest as part of their curriculum.

How to Participate: Small groups of two to six students, and large groups of seven or more (a group also can be an entire class with teacher supervision) submit space settlement designs and related materials to NASA. Teams are judged in the following categories: individual, Grades 6–9; small team, Grades 6–9; large team, Grades 6–9; individual, Grades 10–12; small team, Grades 10–12; and large team, Grades 10–12. Submissions must relate to orbital colonies and must be submitted in hard copy to the contact person listed above.

Cost: If division winners choose to tour the NASA Ames Research Center, they will bear all costs for that trip.

Categories/Content Areas: Science/Astronomy/Engineering/ Technology

Ages/Grade Levels: Grades 6–12

Status: International

Time Commitment: Varies with each group. Entries are to be submitted by late March.

Resources Needed: Entry form, hard copy of work to be submitted

Awards/Benefits: All participants receive a certificate. The grand prize winner has his or her design placed on the NASA Ames Web site. Division winners will be invited to tour the NASA Ames Research Center.

National Achievement Scholarship Program

Web Site: http://www.nationalmerit.org
Description: This academic competition was established in 1964 to provide recognition for outstanding Black American high school students. Black students may enter both the National Achievement Program and the National Merit Program by taking the Preliminary Scholastic Aptitude Test/National Merit Scholarship Qualifying Test (PSAT/NMSQT) and meeting other published requirements for participation. The two annual programs are conducted concurrently but operated and funded separately. A student's standing is determined independently in each program. Black American students can qualify for recognition and be honored as scholars in both the National Merit Program and the National Achievement Program but can receive only one monetary award from National Merit Scholarship Corporation.
How to Participate: To participate in the National Achievement Scholarship Program, a student must do the following:

Take the PSAT/NMSQT in the specified year of the high school program and no later than the third year in Grades 9–12, regardless of grade classification or educational pattern

Request entry to the National Achievement Program by marking the specific space provided on the PSAT/NMSQT answer sheet, thereby identifying him- or herself as a Black American who wishes to be considered in this competition as well as in the National Merit Scholarship Program; be enrolled full-time as a high school student, progressing normally toward graduation or completion of high school, and planning to enroll full-time in college no later than the fall following completion of high school; and be a citizen of the United States; or be a U.S. lawful permanent resident (or have applied for permanent residence, the application for which has not been denied) and intend to become a U.S. citizen at the earliest opportunity allowed by law.

Cost: Unspecified
Categories/Content Areas: Academic
Ages/Grade Levels: Grades 9–12
Status: National; information on regional competitions can be found at the Web site listed above.
Time Commitment: Contests are held in December, February, March, and April. Preparation time varies; the contest takes three days.
Resources Needed: Registration for the test is done by high school rather than individual student. Interested students should see their

counselor at the beginning of the school year to make arrangements to take the PSAT/NMSQT at the school in October.
Awards/Benefits: $2,500 National Merit Scholarships, school scholarships, and corporate scholarships

National African American History Academic Challenge Bowl

Web Site: http://www.100blackmen.org
Description: This national competition is held annually. Questions used in the event come from the work of both Lerone Bennett, Jr., and Dr. Benjamin Quarles.
How to Participate: The competition is part of the national convention of 100 Black Men of America, Inc. In March, students earn the right to compete on the national level by winning their local chapters' competition. There are chapters in each state.
Cost: Unspecified
Categories/Content Areas: History
Ages/Grade Levels: The Junior Division includes teams of students who have not yet entered the ninth grade. The Senior Division includes teams whose members have entered the ninth grade but whose graduation from high school will be no earlier than January of the year of the competition.
Status: Unspecified
Time Commitment: Unspecified
Resources Needed: Unspecified
Awards/Benefits: $250 U.S. Savings Bond and an all-expenses-paid trip to Miami, Florida.

National American Indian Science and Engineering Fair

Web Site: http://www.aises.org
Description: The National American Indian Science and Engineering Fair offers great opportunities for fifth- through twelfth-grade students to win cash prizes and scholarships. In addition, the exposure and experience students gain stay with them as they progress through their college and professional careers.
How to Participate: An outline of the rules and regulations can be found on http://www.aises.org
Cost: $35 per member, $70 for late registration
Categories/Content Areas: Science/Engineering
Ages/Grade Levels: Grades 5–12

Status: National
Time Commitment: The first contest takes place in December. Contest 2 occurs in February, Contest 3 is in March, and Contest 4 is in April. The All-Star contest occurs in May.
Resources Needed: Registration forms. Schools must be members of the National American Indian Science and Engineering Fair K–12 Affiliated Schools Program, and students must have a tribal affiliation/ membership. Adult (teacher) sponsorship also is required.
Awards/Benefits: Cash prizes and scholarships. Top-scoring students at each school receive a ribbon, and each participant receives two Sudoku books.

National Beta Club Convention

Contact: National Beta Club Convention, 151 Beta Club Way, Spartanburg, SC 29306-3012. Phone: 800-845-8281. Fax: 864-542-9300.
Web Site: http://www.betaclub.org
Description: The Beta Club holds state conventions in eighteen states as well as a national convention for high school juniors and seniors. Each convention offers academic competitions, special talent performances, and a Quiz Bowl competition.
How to Participate: Participants must be members of the Beta Club through their school. Clubs participate in state conventions, and the first- and second-place finishers in each category are invited to attend the national convention competition and run for office.
Cost: $13 student registration
Categories/Content Areas: Spelling, Creative Writing, Oratory/ Language Arts, Mathematics, Social Studies, Speech
Ages/Grade Levels: Secondary school students
Status: National
Time Commitment: Four days in the summer
Resources Needed: A sponsor
Awards/Benefits: An awards ceremony is held on the last night of the national convention, and scholarship awards are presented. First-place winners receive $10,000, second-place winners receive $8,000, third-place winners receive $6,000, and fourth-place winners receive $4,000. Also, each state awards several $1,000 scholarships.

National Biblical Greek Exam

Contact: National Biblical Greek Exam, P.O. Box 8473, Moscow, ID 83483. Phone: 800-445-2456. E-mail: nbge@biblicalgreek.org
Web Site: http://www.greekexam.com

Description: This Biblical Greek standardized test is administered online and ranks students and classes nationally. This test allows students to document their understanding of Biblical Greek, which can help students attain advance placement college credit.

How to Participate: Participants should visit the competition's Web site and open an account. Students may then take the online examinations as frequently as they wish.

Cost: $10 for each examination. This fee includes a detailed analysis and ranking of results. There is no limit to the number of times participants may take the examination.

Categories/Content Areas: Greek/Foreign Language

Ages/Grade Levels: Grades 7–12

Status: National

Time Commitment: Varies with each test-taker

Resources Needed: $10 entry fee and a computer with Internet access

Awards/Benefits: Students gain an opportunity to become nationally ranked and determine what they need to study to improve their Biblical Greek.

National Canon Envirothon

Web Site: http://www.envirothon.org

Description: This is an environmental competition offered to high school students in the United States. Teams train by participating in a year long curriculum that concludes in a five-day competition hosted by a different state each year. This competition is designed to test students' knowledge about the environment. Teams are evaluated on soil/land use, aquatic ecology, forestry, wildlife, and a current environmental issue. The competition involves written and oral testing.

How to Participate: Interested students should look through the judging criteria and scoring and the sample tests provided on the Web site listed above. These will help students familiarize themselves with the contest, the year's competition location, and the topic. Students then locate their state/provincial Envirothon through the Web site to register and view the rules and regulations for their specific state/province. Once students have registered, they will receive competition materials.

Cost: Varies

Categories/Content Areas: Environment/Public Speaking

Ages/Grade Levels: Secondary school

Status: National

Time Commitment: Substantial: one year of training and five days of competition during the summer. Registration dates vary by state.

Resources Needed: Registration materials, curriculum, and a team advisor. Note that the rules and procedures, registration dates, and requirements may vary by state.

Awards/Benefits: Scholarships and Canon products will be awarded to teams placing in first through tenth places as well as to volunteer advisors and conservation districts/forestry associations whose teams place in the top ten. Teams who place in the top ten will also receive a trophy or plaque. A nonmonetary award is given to the team that achieves the highest score on the written test for each of the five categories and the preliminary oral examination. The Envirothon Extra Mile award is given to the team that demonstrates the most spirit, cooperation, leadership, and friendship. A Rookie Team Award is presented to the highest scoring team representing a state that has not participated before.

National Catholic Forensic League Grand National Speech and Debate Tournament

Contact: National Catholic Forensic League Grand National Speech and Debate Tournament, 1722 Jefferson St., New London, WI 54953. Phone: 920-982-8420, Extension 1040, and 920-982-3128. E-mail: rsteinho@ newlondon.k12.wi.us.

Web Site: http://www.ncfl.org

Description: This is a two-day speech and debate competition for high school students. Over 2,000 students compete in nine categories of public speaking.

How to Participate: Participants must be members of their local National Catholic Forensic League. Each local league creates its own criteria. Interested students should visit the Web site listed above to view each local league's criteria.

Cost: $35 fee for each participant

Categories/Content Areas: Speech

Ages/Grade Levels: Grades 9–12

Status: United States and Canada

Time Commitment: The competition occurs in late May and lasts two days. Preparation time varies.

Resources Needed: Entry fee, membership in the local National Catholic Forensic League, and two days for the national competition if the student qualifies on the basis of his or her local league criteria.

Awards/Benefits: In speech events, the top twenty-four students receive trophies and medals. The top six will be recognized individually. In debate events, the top four teams receive trophies. In Student Congress, all semifinalists receive medals, and all finalists receive trophies. All students receive a certificate of participation. Some sweepstakes awards are given out.

National Consumers League: LifeSmarts

Contact: Lisa Hertzberg, Program Director, LifeSmarts. Phone: 202-835-3323. E-mail: lisah@nclnet.org.
Web Site: http://www.lifesmarts.org
Description: The LifeSmarts program is a team-based competition for high school students (Grades 9–12) that tests knowledge of consumer rights and responsibilities, current events, environmental issues, personal finance, and technology.
How to Participate: Competition begins with three levels of online contests. Participants initially play as individuals; however, each must have an adult coach who signs on first using a team code. Coaches may register more than one team. Participants may compete on only one team. The face-to-face competitions require teams of four or more. Teams do not have to be affiliated with a school, and team members are not required to be from a single source. Successful state-level teams may go on to compete at the national level.
Cost: There is no cost to participate. Teams that advance to face-to-face competition may be responsible for their own travel expenses.
Categories/Content Areas: Consumer Rights and Responsibilities/Current Events/Environmental Issues/Personal Finance/Technology
Ages/Grade Levels: Grades 9–12
Status: District, state, and national
Time Commitment: Competitions are conducted in September through April. Preparation time varies by individual.
Resources Needed: Participants must have access to a computer with Internet access and have an adult coach. Tips and other information are provided for participants and coaches on the Web site listed above.
Awards/Benefits: Winners and their coaches attend a luncheon and awards ceremony.

National Council on Economic Education and Goldman Sachs Foundation Economics Challenge

Web Site: http://www.economicschallenge.ncee.net
Description: This quiz bowl format competition is a daylong contest of students' knowledge of economics and finance. Participants compete as individuals and teams on the following topics: Macroeconomics, Microeconomics, Current Events/Economic Applications, and International Economics. There are two divisions: (1) the Adam Smith Division and (2) the David Ricardo Division. Teams are to have four members; however, a three-member team may compete. In each division, the first three twenty-minute competition rounds allow

participants to respond to fifteen 5-option multiple-choice questions. The content covered in the competition rounds are as follows: Round I: Microeconomics, Round II: Macroeconomics, and Round III: International Economics and Current Events. In the first two rounds, members compete as individuals, and the team score for the round is the sum of the top three individual scores. In the third round, members compete as a team and submit an answer sheet. Scoring in each round awards ten points for each correct response, deducts five points for each incorrect response, and does not award or deduct points for not responding. The Round III score is weighted equally with each of the first two rounds. The final round is a timed quiz bowl playoff on all topics of economics. The round is between the two highest scoring teams in each division after Rounds I–III. There are thirty questions in the final round, and it concludes when one team has more points than there are questions remaining. Although participants may use pencils and paper during each round, the use of books, notes, calculators, or other support materials is prohibited.

Thirty-five states conduct state-level competitions for each division during February, March, and April. Participating states send a team from each division to the appropriate regional competition: East Region, Midwest Region, Heartland Region, or West Region. Each regional division competition winner competes for the national championship.

How to Participate: To be eligible to participate, a student must be enrolled for credit in a qualifying high school course. The David Ricardo Division is for students enrolled in one-semester (or less) general economics courses or courses that address introductory economic concepts and are taught by a secondary teacher. Participation in this division is limited to one time only. In following years, a participant must compete in the Adam Smith Division. The Adam Smith Division is for students who are enrolled in advanced placement, international baccalaureate, honors, two-semester or advanced economics courses taught by a secondary teacher to students who earn college credit, and to those who are home-schooled. Students who have taken or are taking economics courses for college credit from a postsecondary instructor are not eligible to compete.

Cost: No fee, and most travel expenses for the regional and national competitions are paid by the National Council on Economic Education.

Categories/Content Areas: Monetary Policy and Economic Conditions

Ages/Grade Levels: Secondary school

Status: State, regional, and national

Time Commitment: In addition to the competitions, participant preparation time is required.

Resources Needed: Registration materials and other materials are provided by the National Council on Economic Education

Awards/Benefits: At the regional level, winners and their teachers each receive a $1,000 U.S. Savings Bond, and the runner-up teams and their teachers each receive a $500 U.S. Savings Bond. The winning teams advance to the national competition. National championship teams and their teachers each receive a $3,000 U.S. Savings Bond, and the runner-up teams and their teachers each receive a $1,500 U.S. Savings Bond.

National Engineering Design Challenge (Javits-Wagner-O'Day/ Junior Engineering Technical Society)

Contact: Phone: 703-548-5387, Extension 104. E-mail: nedc@jets.org.
Web Site: http://www.jets.org
Description: This challenge is designed for high school students to help people with disabilities advance or enter the workplace. It is a cross-curricular activity involving problem solving, math, science, research, writing, presentation, and drafting and design skills. This challenge not only applies skills learned in a classroom, but it also can raise social awareness.
How to Participate: Participants must form a team, register, and then participate in an online Scavenger Hunt and identify the problem their team will solve (Round I). Teams that are selected to compete in Round II will build a prototype and submit a written report to be considered for the national finals. Teams that advance to Round III will refine their prototype and report and compete in Washington, DC.
Cost: None
Categories/Content Areas: Problem Solving/Mathematics/Science/ Literary Arts/Design and Drafting
Ages/Grade Levels: Grades 9–12
Status: United States, Puerto Rico, and Guam
Time Commitment: Registration begins in September. The national finals are held in Washington, DC, in February.
Resources Needed: Team; mentor; registration form, which can be found online at the Web site listed above; complementary software, which is optional; Internet access
Awards/Benefits: Finalist teams win an all-expenses-paid trip to the national competition. The best overall design wins $3,000 for the team's sponsoring department. Second- and third-place teams each receive $1,500 for their team's sponsoring department. Each member of each finalist team receives a $50 gift certificate to the Discovery Store.

National Federation of Press Women
High School Communications Contest

Contact: National Federation of Press Women, P.O. Box 5556, Arlington, VA 22205. Phone: 800-780-2715. Fax: 703-812-4555. E-mail: presswomen @aol.com.
Web Site: http://www.nfpw.org
Description: Participants in the competition submit entries in one or more of seventy-eight categories that are grouped by entry type: Print Media, Photography, Radio/Television, World Wide Web, Advertising, Print Media Advertising, Electronic Media Advertising, Public Relations/Promotion/Publicity, Communications Programs and Campaigns, Public Relations Printed Materials, Information for the Media, Speeches, Collegiate, Achievement/Research, and Books/ Fiction/Verse. Entry guidelines vary by type of work. Each entry must have been published, issued, broadcast, printed, or e-published within a given period to be considered in this competition. State and at-large competition winners are forwarded to the national competition for judging.
How to Participate: Members of the National Federation of Press Women may submit entries to the state or the at-large contest director. At-large entries should be sent to Pam Stallsmith, 6532 W. Franklin St., Richmond, VA 23226; pstallsmith@timesdispatch.com.
Cost: National Federation of Press Women dues
Categories/Content Areas: Written and Oral Communication Skills
Ages/Grade Levels: High school
Status: State or at-large and national
Time Commitment: Varies depending on the media and the individual
Resources Needed: Published material that meets the criteria for submission
Awards/Benefits: First-, second-, and third-place winners and honorable mention winners are recognized at the national and state levels. At the national level, first-place winners receive a plaque and $250, and the first and second runners-up receive $150 and $100, respectively. The affiliate with the highest number of points in the national contest receives $100.

National Forensic League
National Tournament

Contact: National Forensic League, National Secretary, P.O. Box 38, Ripon, WI 54971. Phone: 414-748-6206.
Web Site: http://www.nflonline.org

Description: This contest evaluates proficiency in the forensic arts: debate, public speaking, and interpretation. The national tournament includes a Public Forum Debate, a Policy Debate, a Lincoln–Douglas Debate, International Extemporaneous Speaking, United States Extemporaneous Speaking, Original Oratory, Dramatic Interpretation, Humorous Interpretation, and Duo Interpretation.

How to Participate: Registration must be made on the official form signed by the principal, speech instructor, and student and postmarked no later than the date selected by the executive council. Qualification for the national tournament is determined by the number of contestants or teams actually participating in each event at the National Forensic League District Tournament. Four to eleven entries in an event qualifies one contestant or team; twelve to thirty-seven in an event qualifies two contestants or teams; thirty-eight or more in an event qualifies three contestants or teams. In team debate, four to nine teams qualifies one team; ten to twenty-nine qualifies two teams, and thirty or more qualifies three teams. Students must have attended a secondary school fewer than nine semesters; they must be members of the National Forensic League to enter the national tournament. A student may qualify in a maximum of two events. Students may qualify in both categories of debate: interpretation or extemporaneous.

Cost: The entry fee is established each year by the executive council.

Categories/Content Areas: Policy Debate, Values Debate, Legislative Debate, United States Extemporaneous Speaking, Foreign Extemporaneous Speaking, Original Oratory, Dramatic Interpretation, Humorous Interpretation, Commentary, Impromptu Speaking, Prose Reading, Poetry Reading, Expository Speaking/Social Studies, and Speech

Ages/Grade Levels: Secondary school

Status: National

Time Commitment: Applications terminate each June 30 but may be renewed annually.

Resources Needed: Official entry form

Awards/Benefits: Each time a student appears in a debate or main event contest, his or her school receives one trophy point. Trophy points accumulate from year to year, and the participating school with the largest total at the conclusion of each tournament receives the Bruno E. Jacob award.

Each time a student appears in a debate or main event contest, he or she receives one trophy point. Each legislative day of Congress shall count two points; the Super Congress shall count four points, and winning one of the top six awards counts three points. The school with the largest total is awarded the Sweepstakes Trophy and its coach is designated Coach of the Year.

National French Contest
(*Le Grand Concours*)

Contact: Lisa Narug, National Director; P.O. Box 3283; St. Charles, IL 60174-3282. Phone: 630-677-2594. Fax: 630-208-8189. E-mail: legrand-concours@sbglobal.net.

Web Site: http://www.frenchteachers.org

Description: *Le Grand Concours* is sponsored by the American Association of Teachers of French. Competitions are held at the local chapter, regional, and national levels. Areas addressed include listening, speaking, vocabulary, grammar, culture, cultural sensitivity, and civilization. There are two competitions: (1) Foreign Language in the Elementary Schools, for students in Grades 1–6, and (2) Secondary, for students in Grades 7–12. Within each competition, students are assigned to levels on the basis of their grade level and the level of their French language accomplishment.

How to Participate: Teachers wishing to have their student participate must register and purchase the test materials. Students are assigned to competition levels based on their grade level and the level of French language skill.

Cost: Published costs cover the national expenses associated with test and tape development, duplication, and distribution. Chapters may add fees to the published amounts to cover contest expenses. Foreign Language in the Elementary Schools examinations are sold in kits of printed and taped material for ten students. Kit A is $16, Kit B is $18, and listening comprehension CDs are $6 each. Secondary examinations are sold individually for $1.35 to $2.70 each, and listening comprehension CDs are $6 each. Practice tests and CDs also are available for purchase.

Categories/Content Areas: French/Foreign Language

Ages/Grade Levels: Elementary and secondary

Status: Local chapter, regional, and national

Time Commitment: The examination is sixty minutes long. Preparation time may vary.

Resources Needed: For testing, CDs and printed materials are required. Review materials are available at additional cost.

Awards/Benefits: Chapter and national-level awards are given to the top scorers at each level and division. Medals of honor, pins, and certificates are available for purchase to use at the local level.

National Geography Bee

Contact: National Geographic Society; 1145 17th St., NW; Washington, DC 20036. Phone: 202-828-6659.

Web Site: http://www.nationalgeographic.com

Description: The National Geography Bee, a program of the National Geographic Society, is a nationwide contest for schools and home school associations. The contest is for students in Grades 4–8, and there must be at least six participants per grade level. The first two levels of competition are administered at the school level; an invitation to the state-level competition is based on performance on these.

How to Participate: The school principal submits a letter requesting the test materials for the school and a check or money order to cover the registration fee of $60. Principals of schools not previously registered may request registration by writing to the National Geographic Society at the address listed above. Schools in the United States, the District of Columbia, Guam, Puerto Rico, American Samoa, the Northern Mariana Islands, the U.S. Virgin Islands, and Department of Defense Schools are eligible to participate.

Eligibility rules are as follows:

The school level is open to all registered schools; registration ends October 15.

Qualifying-level students must win the school competition.

State-level students must place in the top one hundred scores on the qualifying test.

National-level students must win the state competition.

Students who are prior winners of first-place college scholarships in the National Geography Bee are ineligible, as are members of the immediate families of National Geographic Society employees.

Cost: $60 registration fee
Categories/Content Areas: Geography/Social Studies
Ages/Grade Levels: Grades 4–8
Status: Local, state, and national
Time Commitment: Dates of competition are as follows:

School level: mid-December to mid-January. Qualifying tests must be mailed to the National Geographic Society and postmarked by specified dates. No faxes.

State level: late March or early April

National level: late May

Resources Needed: Official test materials and registration letter and fee. The test materials include an instruction booklet, question booklet, a medal for the school winner, and the qualifying test that must be administered to the school winner. On the basis of their performance on the qualifying test, the top one hundred students in each state are invited to the state-level competition.

Awards/Benefits: At the school level, participants receive a certificate and a prize as well as a certificate and prize for the school. At the qualifying level, participants receive an invitation to participate in state competition. At the state level, first place receives $100, a prize, and a trip to Washington, DC; second place receives $75 and a prize; third place receives $50 and a prize. All students get T-shirts and certificates; schools of the top three winners also get prizes.

At the national level, first place receives a $25,000 college scholarship, second place receives a $15,000 college scholarship, third place receives a $10,000 college scholarship, and the top 10 finalists receive $500 each. Schools of top ten winners also get prizes.

National German Test

Contact: American Association of German Teachers; 112 Haddontowne Ct., No. 104; Cherry Hill, NJ 08034-3668. Phone: 856-795-5553.
Web Site: http://www.astg.com
Description: This competition evaluates achievement in the acquisition of the German language. This first level is a series of tests that are administered to students in Levels II, III, and IV language classes. The second level of competition is restricted to students who score above the 90th percentile on the first tests. Tests are sent to participating schools for administration by school personnel. The tests assess listening comprehension, reading and conversational skills, grammar and idioms, and reading comprehension. Students who score above the 90th percentile are eligible to apply for a study trip to Germany.
How to Participate: Participating schools receive the necessary test materials from the American Association of Teachers of German for the school-level and qualifying tests. Tests are given during a designated testing period, and answer sheets must be returned by a deadline.
Cost: $5 per test/per student, with a minimum order of $20. Other materials to help students prepare for the examinations (books, tapes, and software) are available for purchase.
Categories/Content Areas: German/Foreign Language
Ages/Grade Levels: Tests are suitable for students in the middle of their second, third, and fourth year of high school German.
Status: National
Time Commitment: Each test takes approximately one hour and five minutes. Preparation time is up to the individual teacher and student. The test administration period lasts from mid-December to the end of January. The deadline to return answer sheets is the last day of the testing period.

Resources Needed: Although teachers may keep the tests they order for their students each year, sample copies of the tests from the previous two years and cassettes for Levels II, III, and IV are available for purchase. Other resources are for optional purchase.

Awards/Benefits: Students who score at or above the 90th percentile can apply for the monthlong travel–study program, all expenses paid, to Germany. The winner lives with a German family for four weeks; takes classes in a Nurnberger Gymnasium; and takes trips to Munich, Wurzburg, and Berlin. Most chapters also hold award ceremonies to honor the students who score at or above the 90th percentile. Often, book and cash prizes are donated by local German-American groups; the embassies and consulates of Austria, Germany, and Switzerland; and the Goethe Institutes, among others.

National Greek Examination

Contact: Deb Davies, Chair; ACL/NJCL (American Classical League/National Junior Classical League); National Greek Examination; 123 Argilla Rd.; Andover, MA 01810-4622. Phone: 978-749-9446. E-mail: ddavies@brooksschool.org.

Web Site: http://www.nge.aclclassics.org

Description: This examination, offered by the American Classical League, assesses knowledge of the Greek language for students of first-, second-, and third-year high school Greek, or the college equivalent courses. The National Greek Examination is a series of six examinations, including Attic Greek examinations, Introduction, Beginning, Intermediate, Prose, and Tragedy, and a Homeric Greek examination. Examinations are administered at the participant's school and returned for scoring. Passages printed in the Homeric, Attic Greek, and Modern Greek examinations are treated as sight passages.

How to Participate: For a student to participate, a teacher must submit an application, a request for the tests. Applications and payment of the fee must be postmarked by the specified deadline, typically in early January. Examinations are mailed by the end of February to the school principal or department chair. Simultaneously, a postcard of notification that the exams are en route is mailed to the teacher who submitted the application.

Cost: $5 per examination plus $10 for handling the order. Individual examinations from previous years are available for $2 each. To order, contact: ACL/NJCL National Greek Examination, The American Classical League, Miami University, 422 Wells Mill Dr., Oxford, OH 45056. Phone: 513-529-7741. Fax: 513-529-7742. E-mail: info@aclclassics.org.

Categories/Content Areas: Greek/Foreign Language

Ages/Grade Levels: High school or college/university students of the first-year and elementary Greek (Level 1), or second-year and intermediate Greek (Level 2), or third-year and advanced Greek (Level 3)
Status: National
Time Commitment: Each examination takes fifty minutes and has forty multiple-choice questions. Preparation time is at the discretion of the participant.
Resources Needed: Only the examination is required. Copies of past examinations are available and may be helpful as study guides or aids.
Awards/Benefits: Purple, blue, red, and green ribbons are given for outstanding performances on the examinations. High school seniors who earn purple or blue ribbons may apply for a $1,000 scholarship. Scholarship recipients must earn six credits of Greek or Latin during the school year. Winners are selected by the National Latin Exam/ National Greek Examination scholarship committee. Teachers of eligible students receive application forms in the mail by early April. Winners are announced at the American Classical League Institute and notified directly by mail.

National High School Oratorical Contest

Contact: National High School Oratorical Contest, P.O. Box 1055, Indianapolis, IN 46206-1055. Phone: 317-630-1249. E-mail: acy@legion .org.
Web Site: http://www.legion.org
Description: This contest is designed to aid high school students in developing deeper knowledge about and a greater appreciation of the U.S. Constitution.
How to Participate: Each state organization of the American Legion may send one statewide participant to the national division competition. For local information, students should contact their local American Legion post. Students prepare a planned oration about some aspect of the U.S. Constitution with a focus on the duties and obligations of citizens.
Costs: The American Legion bears the cost for the department winners' travel and lodging to the national contest along with a chaperone.
Categories/Content Areas: Speech
Ages/Grade Levels: Grades 9–12
Status: National
Time Commitment: Varies depending on state and advancement
Resources Needed: Oratory skills, a chaperone, and nomination from the participant's statewide competition.
Awards/Benefits: $1,500 scholarships are awarded to each state (department) winner. The first-place winner at the national level

receives a scholarship of $18,000, the second-place winner receives $16,000, and the third-place winner receives $14,000.

National High School Student Solar Design Contest

Contact: Richard E. Deutschmann, PRSEA-NSDC (Potomac Region Solar Energy Association National High School Solar Design Contest), 9486 Cameldriver Ct., Columbia, MD 21045.
Web Site: http://www.prsea.org
Description: This contest is designed for high school age students who want to apply the principles of solar energy in new ways. Students can improve on an existing solar device or design an entirely new one. Participants can enter as individuals or as teams of up to four.
How to Participate: Participants must submit an entry form that includes a title page listing the project title, an abstract, the sponsoring teacher, high school name, student's name, student's Social Security Number, and student's home address. Participants must also submit a description of the project that does not exceed two pages. Submission of a design plan is also required. The descriptions should include the design's function and purpose and the need the design meets.
Cost: Cost of materials used.
Categories/Content Areas: Science
Ages/Grade Levels: High school
Status: National
Time Commitment: Entries must be submitted by late April.
Resources Needed: Entry form, description, design plan
Awards/Benefits: Awards range from trophies to $500.

National History Day

Contact: National History Day, 119 Cecil Hall, University of Maryland, College Park, MD 20742. Phone: 301-314-9739. E-mail: national.history.day@umail.umd.edu.
Web Site: http://www.nationalhistoryday.org
Description: The National History Day competition evaluates students' research, writing, and communication skills in history around an annual theme. Participants enter one of seven categories: (1) Individual Paper, (2) Individual or (3) Group Performance, (4) Individual or (5) Group Exhibit, or (6) Individual or (7) Group Documentary. Groups are composed of two to five participants.

Projects are judged on the basis of their historical quality, clarity of presentation, and relation to the theme. Participants advance to the national competition on the basis of success in local, district, and state competitions.

How to Participate: Individual schools determine the size and scope of the local History Day competition. All National History Day program coordinators are history professionals: social studies teachers, college and university professors, and historical society officials. Professionals such as educators and historians serve as judges at each level of the History Day competition.

Cost: None

Categories/Content Areas: History/Social Studies

Ages/Grade Levels: Junior Division (Grades 6–8) and Senior Division (Grades 9–12)

Status: Local, state, national

Time Commitment: Four days in June

Resources Needed: Materials necessary to complete the selected project. Supplemental materials such as the *National History Day Student Contest Guide* and *Judges' Handbook* are available on request from National History Day to help teachers and students prepare for the contest. The materials may be duplicated for classroom use.

Awards/Benefits: Certificates, medals, trophies, monetary awards, and special prizes are used to recognize winners. The top national winners receive awards as follows: Gold medal winners receive $1,000, silver medal winners receive $500, and bronze medal winners receive $250. The gold medal winning projects in the Senior Division Individual and Group Documentary categories receive The History Channel Award of $5,000 in lieu of the $1,000 award. In addition, two awards are given to teachers for their work related to National History Day. The Outstanding History Educator Award recipient receives $5,000 and a special plaque, and the Richard M. Farrell Teacher of Merit Award recipient receives $1,000 and plaque of recognition.

National Latin Exam

Contact: National Latin Exam, University of Mary Washington, 1301 College Ave., Fredericksburg, VA 22401. E-mail: nle@umw.edu.

Web Site: http://www.nle.org

Description: Sponsored by the American Classical League and the National Junior Classical League, this examination assesses students' knowledge of Latin. Any student enrolled in Latin I, II, III, IV, or V is eligible to take the exam. There are five categories—Introduction to Latin, Latin I, Latin II, Latin III–IV Poetry, and Latin V–VI—from which each student may select the appropriate examination.

Examinations are administered at the participant's school and mailed in for scoring. They are not based on a textbook series. A packet including awards, a printout of student scores, national norms, and an answer key for all examinations is mailed to the relevant Latin teacher about five weeks after the examination administration. Each examination is composed of forty multiple-choice questions and is timed.

How to Participate: A school must submit an American Classical League/National Junior Classical League entry form and a check or money order payable to *National Latin Exam* at the address listed above. The examinations are mailed to the school principal in February and are to be administered by school personnel other than the Latin teacher during the second full week in March. Answer sheets are to be mailed in for scoring. Test performance results will be sent to the school in April.

Cost: $4 per student, $10 for a single examination

Categories/Content Areas: Latin/Foreign Language

Ages/Grade Levels: Secondary

Status: Local and national

Time Commitment: Time limit for the examination is forty-five minutes. Preparation time for the examination is up to the individual and the schools participating.

Resources Needed: Schools may want to order the previous examinations and a syllabus.

Awards/Benefits: High school seniors who are gold medal winners in Latin III–IV Prose, Latin III–IV Poetry, or Latin V–VI may apply for $1,000 scholarships. Scholarship recipients must take at least one year of Latin or classical Greek in college. Other awards include special hand-lettered certificates for perfect scorers, a gold medal and summa cum laude certificate for top scorers, a silver medal and maxima cum laude certificate for second-place winners, a magna cum laude certificate for third-place winners, a cum laude certificate for fourth-place winners, Introduction to Latin ribbons, and special certificates of achievement.

National Mythology Exam

Contact: Excellence Through the Classics, 422 Wells Mill Dr., Oxford, OH 45056. Phone: 513-529-7741. E-mail: info@aclclassics.org.

Web Site: http://www.etclassics.org

Description: This examination aims to nurture and support the classics. It was designed to support individuals and organizations dedicated to promoting and advancing the study of the classics.

How to Participate: Participants register for the examination online. Registration material can be found on the Web site listed above.

Cost: There is a $3 entry fee for students within the United States; a $4 entry fee for students outside of the United States; and a $15 registration, shipping, and handling fee.

Categories/Content Areas: Classics/Language Arts

Ages/Grade Levels: Grades 3–9

Status: National

Time Commitment: Varies, but tests are administered from February 19 to March 2. The registration deadline is mid-January.

Resources Needed: Registration form, entry fee, test-taking time; students may want to visit the Web site for sample examination questions.

Awards/Benefits: Gold, silver, and bronze medallions

National Peace Essay Contest

Contact: Heidi E. Schaeffer, National Peace Essay Contest Coordinator; 1550 M Street, NW, Ste. 700; Washington, DC 20005-1708. Phone: 202-429-3846. Fax: 202-429-6063. E-mail: essaycontest .usip.org.

Web Site: http://www.usip.org

Description: The National Peace Essay Contest evaluates research, writing, and reasoning skills related to international peace. There must be a local contest coordinator who reviews essays and serves as the liaison between participants and state and national contest personnel. The local coordinator reviews essays for grammatical and typographical errors and general content. At state and national competitions, essays are evaluated on seven criteria: (1) focus, (2) organization, (3) analysis, (4) conclusions and recommendations, (5) originality, (6) voice, and (7) style and mechanics. Students first compete at the state level. Three national winners are selected from the first-place state competition winners.

How to Participate: The coordinator must contact the National Peace Essay Contest to request contest guidelines. Entries are due in early February. Following topic and essay guidelines, students write and submit essays to the local coordinator, who reviews each essay and forwards it to the state level.

Cost: None

Categories/Content Areas: Language Arts/International Peace/ Social Studies

Ages/Grade Levels: Grades 9–12

Status: State and national

Time Commitment: This depends on the individual contest coordinator. The minimum time commitment for the coordinator would be time spent reading students' essays and filling out the necessary forms. The amount of time spent on the essay is up to the individual student. The contest takes place from September 1 to February 1.

Resources Needed: Guidebook, which includes the contest rules, essay topics, entry forms, awards program highlights, and winning essays from previous years

Awards/Benefits: Over 150 scholarships are awarded. The top three essayists in the United States receive college scholarships: $10,000 for first place, $5,000 for second place, and $2,500 for third place. In addition, each first-place state winner receives a scholarship of $1,000 and an all-expenses-paid trip to Washington, DC, for the award program.

National Portuguese Exam

Contact: AATSP (American Association of Teachers of Spanish and Portuguese), 423 Exton Commons, Exton, PA 19341-2451.
Web Site: http://www.aatsp.org
Description: This contest tests students' Portuguese written and oral skills.
How to Participate: Sponsoring schools or teachers order tests and register by e-mailing cowlest@comcast.net
Cost: The sponsoring teacher must be a member of the American Association of Teachers of Spanish and Portuguese. There is a $5 fee.
Categories/Content Areas: Portuguese/Foreign Language
Ages/Grade Levels: Any student, in Grades K–12, registered in a Portuguese class
Status: National
Time Commitment: The examination is administered in the student's school by a teacher and proctor in February/March. The test takes fifty minutes.
Resources Needed: A sponsoring school or teacher, a blank audiocassette tape to be used for testing, and access to a recording device. Students must also currently be enrolled in a Portuguese course.
Awards/Benefits: Each participant receives a certificate. National winners receive a plaque.

National Schools Project Poetry Contest

Contact: National Schools Project, ERC-PMB101, 582 E. Boise Ave., Boise, ID 83706. Phone: 208-363-9173.
Web Site: http://www.youngpoets.org
Description: This contest encourages students to share their writing and provides an opportunity for publication.
How to Participate: Schools may participate by submitting their students' most creative works of poetry. Poems should be no more

than eighty words in length and should be submitted with a submission form found on the Web site listed above.

Cost: None

Categories/Content Areas: Poetry/Language Arts

Ages/Grade Levels: Any student enrolled in a public or private school

Status: National and Canada

Time Commitment: Varies. The submission deadline is in mid-March.

Resources Needed: Submission form, which can be found on the Web site

Awards/Benefits: Winners are published in the *Young American Poetry Digest* and receive a free copy of this publication. Each school that enters qualifies for a $100 or a $50 award for the most students' poems accepted.

National Science Bowl

Contact: Sue Ellen Walbridge, National Science Bowl coordinator. Phone: 202-586-7231. E-mail: sue-ellen.walbridge@science.doe.gov.

Web Site: http://www.scied.science.doe.gov

Description: The bowl is composed of teams that attend science seminars and compete in a verbal forum where they solve technical problems and answer science and math questions. The regional and national competitions aim to encourage involvement in math and science and improve awareness about careers in science and technology. There is also a bowl for middle school students.

How to Participate: On the National Science Bowl Web site, students can find the rules and regulations, sample questions, and a list of regional competitions so they can locate a nearby competition. There will be a link for that competition, and the team's coach can begin the registration process. Registration procedures depend on the region, but most sites allow online registration. Teams consist of four students and may also include one alternate. Students compete in their regional bowl, and the winner of each regional bowl is invited to the National Science Bowl in Washington, DC.

Cost: None

Categories/Content Areas: Science/Math/Technology

Ages/Grade Levels: Grades 9–12 and students under age 20 or those who receive a special waiver from the Department of Energy

Status: National

Time Commitment: The National Bowl takes place in April/May in Washington, DC. Regional deadlines and dates vary, so coaches should check with their regional bowl or bowl director. The middle school division takes place in Colorado in June.

Resources Needed: Teams of four or five students and a coach

Awards/Benefits: The winner from each region is invited to attend the national event in Washington, DC, in April/May. The team's expenses are covered.

National Science Decathlon

Contact: general_questions@sciencedecathlon.com
Web Site: http://www.sciencedecathlon.com
Description: Each decathlon tournament is made up of ten team events and up to four pilot events. Teams are entered in one of two divisions: (1) Division A, for ninth- to twelfth-grade students, and (2) Division B, for sixth- to ninth-grade junior high, middle school, and intermediate elementary students. Teams may be divided into smaller pairings during tournaments to compete in the various events.
How to Participate: Students are encouraged to compete in teams, although they are not required to do so. Teams comprise up to five students and up to two alternates. Teams and their schools must register and pay a registration fee.
Cost: $85 registration fee per team. School registration is $145.
Categories/Content Areas: Science
Ages/Grade Levels: Grades 6–12
Status: National
Time Commitment: Tournament dates vary according to conference.
Resources Needed: Registration form and fee, a team, and a coach. Participants should view the rules and regulations found on the Web site listed above and check back for updates.
Awards/Benefits: Ribbons, medals, and trophies are given to winning teams, individuals, and coaches.

National Science Olympiad

Contact: Science Olympiad, Inc.; 2 Trans Am Plaza Drive, Ste. 415; Oakbrook Terrace, IL 60181. Phone: 630-792-1287. Fax: 630-792-1287.
Web Site: http://www.soinc.org
Description: The National Science Olympiad has four competitive divisions according to grade level and some noncompetitive events for Grades K–12. Questions evaluate science knowledge and concepts, science processes and thinking skills, and science application and technology. Teams of participants in Grades 9–12 may advance to state and national tournaments.
How to Participate: A school registers teams by the entry deadline according to the grade and subject categories listed above. There is no limit to the number of students who may participate.
Cost: Division A1 (Grades K–3) is $12, Division A2 (Grades 3–6) is $20, Division B (Grades 6–9) is $60, Division C (Grades 9–12) is $60

Categories/Content Areas: Science
Ages/Grade Levels: Grades K–12
Status: Local, state, and national
Time Commitment: One class period plus preparation time
Resources Needed: An official registration form, available from the above address
Awards/Benefits: Each team a school registers receives eleven awards: one medal and ten certificates. There are also individual and team awards awarded on the national level.

National Society of Black Engineers Try-Math-A-Lon Competition

Web Site: http://www.nsbe.org
Description: Try-Math-A-Lon (TMAL) is a tutoring program meant to foster good study habits, help prepare for standardized test examinations such as the ACT and SAT, and promote competition and good sportsmanship. The TMAL competition is held between teams composed of high school students in Grades 9–12. The purpose of the competition is to help groom TMAL team members for success in science, technology, engineering, and mathematics courses and prepare them for standardized (SAT/ACT) testing.

The aim of the National Society of Black Engineers (NSBE) is for each TMAL team to compete in a local competition held in a local NSBE zone in order to advance to the Fall Regional Conference TMAL competition to compete. Winning local teams from each zone go on to compete at the regional TMAL competition held in each of the six NSBE regions, at the Fall Regional Conference. The winning regional TMAL teams go on to compete for the TMAL World national competition title.

How to Participate: Every TMAL team must meet the following criteria:

Consist of four members and an optional alternate

Be a combination of students in Grades 9–12 (TMAL teams cannot consist of four seniors)

Be paid NSBE junior members

Be a member of a registered TMAL team with coach who is a current NSBE member

Register with the regional TMAL coordinator

Please contact the national TMAL coordinator at pci@nsbe-ae.org to get the contact information for your regional coordinator.
Cost: None. TMAL funding is provided by gifts and volunteering to NSBE.

Categories/Content Areas: TMAL questions are written with the curricula for Grades 9–12 in mind. In addition, many problems are designed to challenge and accelerate student learning, and questions become progressively more difficult at each level of the TMAL competition.

Math, science, and engineering topics include Algebra and Functions; Data Analysis, Statistics and Probability; Geometry and Measurements; Numbers and Operations; Problem Solving; Real World Engineering Questions; African American Inventors; and Scientists and African American First.

Ages/Grade Levels: Grades 9–12

Status: National

Time Commitment: Registration ends in June; training occurs throughout the year from May to March and varies with each team. Local competitions occur in September and October, and regional competition dates vary by each region's conference. The world deadline is in December, and the U.S. deadline is in January. The national competition takes place in late March/early April. Participants should check the Web site listed above for each year's specific dates.

Resources Needed: Permission slips and medical forms, chaperone information sheet, coach information sheet, student information and aptitude survey, TMAL team list entry forms

Awards/Benefits: Trophies and scholarships

National Spanish Exam

Contact: AATSP (American Association of Teachers of Spanish and Portuguese), 423 Exton Commons, Exton, PA 19341-2451.

Web Site: http://www.nationalspanishexam.org

Description: This contest tests students' written and oral Spanish skills. The examination aims to recognize achievement in Spanish study, promote proficiency, and stimulate further learning.

How to Participate: Teachers must fill out the teacher registration form and pay their AATSP dues. Teachers will then be e-mailed a link to the online registration form.

Costs: The sponsoring teacher must be a member of AATSP or pay a nonmember fee of $75. Fees vary with each chapter. The average is $3–$6.

Categories/Content Areas: Spanish/Foreign Language

Ages/Grade Levels: Spanish students in Grades 11–12

Status: National

Time Commitment: The examination is given in the spring, in centrally located test centers.

Resources Needed: Each student must have Internet access. Registration by a teacher and fee payment are required. Practice materials may be found online.

Awards/Benefits: The highest scores are recognized at the state and national levels. National winners are published in the September issue of the AATSP journal and on the National Spanish Examination Web site. Each chapter awards students differently.

National Vocabulary Championship

Web Site: http://www.winwithwords.com

Description: This championship uses competition and word play to engage and reward students while teaching them the value of a strong vocabulary.

How to Participate: Students must first qualify in their citywide championship. This step is an online test. Top scorers will then be invited to take a regionwide test. Fifty finalists win the opportunity to participate in the national competition.

Cost: None

Categories/Content Areas: Vocabulary/Language Arts

Ages/Grade Levels: Secondary

Status: National

Time Commitment: The online test is administered in October and November. Regional finals take place in December.

Resources Needed: Students should locate a citywide competition and have access to the Internet so they can take the online test. The national championship takes place in March.

Awards/Benefits: Citywide competition grand prize winners receive $5,000 toward college tuition, a dictionary, and a trip to New York City to compete in the national finals. Second-prize winners receive a $500 scholarship and $500 in Princeton Review materials. Third-prize winners receive $500 in Princeton Review materials. The citywide grand champion's school also receives various prizes, including a $1,500 grant and $1,500 in Princeton Review materials.

The national grand prize winner receives $40,000 toward his or her college tuition, a dictionary, and $500 in Mead supplies. The second-place winner receives $2,500 in college tuition and $2,500 in Princeton Review materials, and the third-place winner receives $500 toward college tuition and $500 in Princeton Review materials.

National Women's Hall of Fame Essay and New Media Contest

Contact: National Women's Hall of Fame, 76 Fall St., P.O. Box 335, Seneca Falls, NY 13148. Phone: 315-568-8060. E-mail: cmoulton@ greatwomen.org.

Web Site: http://www.greatwomen.org

Description: In each of two divisions, Essay and New Media, participants compete with others in their grade range.

How to Participate: Submit an essay or media document to the address listed above.

Cost: None

Categories/Content Areas: Language Arts

Ages/Grade Levels: Intermediate (Grades 4–6), Junior High School (Grades 7–9), and Senior High School (Grades 10–12)

Time Commitment: Varies by entrant

Resources Needed: None

Awards/Benefits: Awards are given in each category in each grade range.

National Young Astronomer Award

Contact: Astronomical League; National Office Manager; 9201 Ward Pkwy, Ste. 100; Kansas City, MO 64114.

Web Site: http://www.astroleague.org

Description: This award program provides young people with an opportunity to learn astronomy, and it rewards excellence in astronomy.

How to Participate: Participants must submit the application package no later than January 31.

Cost: None

Categories/Content Areas: Science/Astronomy

Ages/Grade Levels: U.S. citizens ages 14–19 who are not enrolled in college by the award deadline

Status: U.S. citizens and foreign students if they are enrolled in a U.S. secondary school on the application deadline

Time Commitment: The submission deadline is in January.

Resources Needed: The application package, which includes an application form, summary of astronomy-related activities, and optional exhibits.

Awards/Benefits: The first-place winner will receive a Meade 10-inch (2.5-cm) LX-200, Schmidt-Cassegrain telescope, valued at about $3,000. The first-place winner also receives an all-expenses-paid trip to attend the national convention to receive his or her award. Second- and third-place winners receive a lifetime membership to the

University of Texas McDonald Observatory. In addition, first-, second-, and third-place winners receive a plaque and publication in various magazines and newsletters.

Nob Yoshigahara Puzzle Design Competition

Web Site: http://www.johnrausch.com
Description: Participants design new, innovative mechanical puzzles. All types of puzzles are accepted for judging, as long as they are a new design or an inventive application of a known principle.
How to Participate: Entries must be received by late June. Check the Web site listed above for the specific date, which may vary from year to year. Two copies of the puzzle, a complete description, and entry fee must be submitted. Participants are limited to three puzzle designs. The entry fee and one copy of the puzzle should be sent to: Nick Baxter, IPP (International Puzzle Party) Design Competition, 801 Newhall Rd., Hillsborough, CA 94010. The second copy of the puzzle should be sent to Brian Young, IPP Design Competition, P.O. Box 37, Tamborine, Queensland 4270, Australia.
Cost: $25 per entry
Categories/Content Areas: Problem Solving/Engineering or Mechanical Skills
Ages/Grade Levels: Open to all
Status: International
Time Commitment: Varies
Resources Needed: Entry fee, complete description, and picture or drawing of the puzzle
Awards/Benefits: The Puzzlers' Award is given to the puzzle that gets the highest overall score. Prizes include trophies, pins, plaques, and certificates. The results of the competition will be reported in the IPP Souvenir Booklet and on the IPP Design Competition Web site.

Odyssey of the Mind

Contact: Carole Micklus, Executive Director; International Headquarters; Creative Competitions, Inc.; 1325 Rt. 130 S., Ste. F; Gloucester, NJ 08030. Phone: 856-456-7776. Fax: 856-456-7008. E-mail: info@odysseyofthe mind.com.
Web Site: http://www.odysseyofthemind.com
Description: Odyssey of the Mind evaluates the products of creative thinking and problem solving involving a wide range of project topics. Teams of up to seven students select and solve a long-term problem in one of five categories following competition guidelines.

Long-term project categories are Vehicle, Technical, Classics, Structure, and Performance. At competitions, teams describe their long-term problem-solving project and present the solution, plus they solve a spontaneous problem. Scoring is based on the long-term problem-solving project, the spontaneous problem-solving project, and style.

How to Participate: To participate, the school or organization must become a member of the Odyssey of the Mind Association.

Costs: $135 for individual school or community group and $100 for additional memberships for the same group

Categories/Content Areas: General Problem Solving

Ages/Grade Levels: Membership is open to kindergarten through college students. Teams are assigned to one of four divisions: Division I (Grades K–5; less than 12 years old), Division II (Grades 6–8; less than 15 years old), Division III (Grades 9–12; less than 19 years old), and Division IV (College; must be a high school graduate enrolled in at least one course at a two- or four-year institution of higher education).

Status: Regional, state, and international

Time Commitment: Long-term problem-solving time and preparation for competition vary at the discretion of the team.

Resources Needed: A variety of books and handbooks are available for purchase. Creative problem-solving activities for primary grades are available for use in classroom instruction.

Members receive a membership packet containing the following: Odyssey of the Mind School curriculum materials, a program handbook, five current competitive long-term problems, a noncompetitive long-term primary-level problem, and a subscription to the Odyssey of the Mind newsletter.

Awards/Benefits: Awards are given at all levels.

Ohio State University Press
The Journal Award in Poetry

Contact: Poetry Editor, The Ohio State University Press, 180 Pressey Hall, 1070 Carmack Rd., Columbus OH 43210-1002.

Web Site: http://www.ohiostatepress.org

Description: Each year, *The Journal*, Ohio State University's literary magazine, selects one full-length manuscript for publication. The manuscript must be original and previously unpublished.

How to Participate: Manuscripts of at least forty-eight typed pages of original, unpublished poetry should be sent to the address listed above.

Cost: $25 nonrefundable handling fee

Categories/Content Areas: Poetry

Ages/Grade Levels: All

Status: National

Time Commitment: Varies. Manuscripts must be postmarked by September.
Resources Needed: Entry fee and mailing materials
Awards/Benefits: Publication and the Charles B. Wheeler $3,000 prize

Olympiad of Spoken Russian

Contact: ACTR (American Council of Teachers of Russian), 1776 Massachusetts Ave., NW, Ste. 700; Washington, DC 20036.
Web Site: http://www.americancouncils.org
Description: This competition gives students an opportunity to demonstrate excellence in Russian and a forum in which to test their knowledge of the language.
How to Participate: Students must be registered by a teacher. Teachers can download forms on the Web site listed above.
Costs: $4 for students of American Council of Teachers of Russian members, $5.50 for nonmembers.
Categories/Content Areas: Russian/Foreign Language
Ages/Grade Levels: Grades 9–12
Status: National
Time Commitment: The Olympiad is held in March or April of each year. State or regional chairpersons should be contacted for details.
Resources Needed: Registration forms and fee
Awards/Benefits: Participants can receive gold, silver, or bronze medals for proficiency. The top students are invited to participate in a study-abroad program in Russia.

Panasonic Academic Challenge

Contact: Academic Competitions Coordinator, Panasonic Academic Challenge, P.O. Box 391, Bartow, FL 33831. Phone: 863-968-5168. Fax: 863-968-5169.
Web Site: http://www.academic-challenge.org
Description: This is an academic competition in the areas of mathematics, science, English, social studies, the fine arts, foreign language, and computer science.
How to Participate: One team of six high school students (four players and two alternates) and a coach is selected to represent each state and U.S. territory. The team selection process varies from state to state. Some states use a state tournament process, and other states choose the team.
Cost: The minimum cost per team to attend the national contest is $2,450. This includes two hotel rooms and some meals.

Categories/Content Areas: Computers, Foreign Language, Language Arts, Mathematics, Science, Social Studies
Ages/Grade Levels: Grades 9–12
Status: National, including U.S. territories
Time Commitment: The Panasonic Academic Challenge lasts for four days in June. Preparation time is at the discretion of the individual teams.
Resources Needed: Application materials
Awards/Benefits: Each member of a team and the coach of the team receive the following: The first-place team receives a $2,500 scholarship and a ring, the second-place team receives a $1,500 scholarship and a ring, and the third-place team receives a $500 scholarship and a ring. A six-member All-America Academic Team is selected from all participants. Each of them receives a $1,000 scholarship and a medallion.

Physics Bowl

Contact: AAPT (American Association of Physics Teachers), One Physics Ellipse, College Park, MD 20740.
Web Site: http://www.aapt.org
Description: This competition is a forty-question, forty-five minute multiple-choice examination designed to encourage interest in physics and to recognize those who excel in it.
How to Participate: Each school must submit an entry form with an entry fee of $12.50 to cover the cost of the tests. The tests are mailed to the school's physics instructor and administered at the school.
Cost: $12.50 fee, borne by the school. Teachers' preparation packets are $19.95 for American Association of Physics Teachers members and $29.95 for nonmembers.
Categories/Content Areas: Science (Physics)
Ages/Grade Levels: Grades 9–12, divided into first- and second-year physics students
Status: National
Time Commitment: The examination is given between April 4 and 18.
Resources Needed: Schools need an entry form and entry fee. There is also an optional preparation packet available for the teachers to prepare their students.
Awards/Benefits: Certificates of participation are awarded to all students and teachers. The top regional school in each division wins a Thirty Go Motion USB Motion Detector with Logger Lite Software as well as a $50 gift certificate from Vernier Software and Technology. Second-place teams win a Thirty Go Motion USB Motion Detector from Vernier Software and Technology. Sixty $100 gift certificates are given by Frey Scientific to the first- and second-place winners in each region. Sixty free memberships in the American Association of Physics

Teachers are given to the schools that place first and second in each region. Finally, the top four students in the top school receive a T-shirt.

President's Environmental Youth Awards

Contact: U.S. Environmental Protection Agency; 1200 Pennsylvania Ave., NW (1701A); Washington, DC 20460.
Web Site: http://www.epa.gov
Description: This program aims to recognize students across the United States for projects that describe their commitment to the environment. Participants submit projects that can cover a wide range of topics, including tree planting programs; recycling programs; and videos, skits, and newsletters that focus on environmental issues and environmental science projects.
How to Participate: This award program involves both a regional certificate program and a national competition. Participants must submit their applications by the deadline. Students should visit the Web site listed above or their regional coordinator for detailed entry information.
Cost: None
Categories/Content Areas: Environment/Problem Solving/Language Arts
Ages/Grade Levels: Grades K–12
Status: National
Time Commitment: The deadline for submitting projects to the regional level is October 31 of each year.
Resources Needed: The application, which can be found online at the Web site listed above. Students may want to visit the Web site to see past winners, entry criteria, submission information, and to locate their region.
Awards/Benefits: All participants will receive a signed certificate from the President of the United States. One outstanding project in each region will be selected to receive a Presidential plaque and to attend an award ceremony sponsored by the Environmental Protection Agency.

Program to Recognize Excellence in Student Literary Magazines

Contact: National Council of Teachers of English, 1111 W. Kenyon Rd., Urbana, IL 61801-1096. Phone: 217-328-3870 and 800-369-NCTE (800-369-6283). Fax: 217-328-0977.
Web Site: http://www.ncte.org

Description: This program ranks school literary publications, not yearbooks or newspapers. Documents are evaluated on the basis of literary quality and design and graphics.

How to Participate: Submit three copies of the entry form and three copies of a magazine published between September of the previous year and July of the entry year along with the entry fee and a self-addressed, stamped postcard if notification of the entry being received is desired.

Cost: $25 entry fee

Categories/Content Areas: Composition/Writing/Language Arts

Ages/Grade Levels: Junior high schools, middle schools, and senior high schools

Status: United States, Canada, and American schools abroad

Time Commitment: The deadline to enter is July 1.

Resources Needed: Official entry form

Awards/Benefits: The initial judging is based on a point system. Schools are notified of ranked magazines but do not receive either critiques or score sheets. Rankings are as follows: Superior = 91–100 points, Excellent = 81–90.9 points, Above Average = 71–80.9 points, Unranked = 70.9 or fewer points.

Promising Young Writers

Contact: Promising Young Writers, 1111 W. Kenyon Rd., Urbana, IL 61801-1096. Phone: 217-278-3608 and 800-369-6283, Extension 3608. E-mail: pyw@ncte.org.

Web Site: http://www.ncte.org

Description: This program was designed to encourage and recognize eighth-grade students' talent in writing. It also aims to emphasize the importance of writing skills.

How to Participate: Students must be nominated by their teachers. The student and representative teacher then fill out and submit the entry form. Students must then submit three sets of papers with one copy of the best writing sample stapled to a copy of the student's impromptu writing piece with a copy of the completed nomination form.

Cost: $5 entry fee

Categories/Content Areas: Language Arts

Ages/Grade Levels: Grade 8

Status: United States, Canada, Virgin Islands, and American students abroad

Time Commitment: Entries and fees are due by late January.

Resources Needed: A "Promising Young Writers" brochure, which includes the entry form, entry fee, and nomination form

Awards/Benefits: All participants receive a certificate and a citation, and winners' names will be posted on the National Council of Teachers of English Web site along with their school name, city, and state.

Prudential Spirit of Community Awards

Contact: Prudential Spirit of Community Awards, 1904 Association Dr., Reston, VA 20191. Phone: 703-860-7324. E-mail: spirit@principles .org.
Web Site: http://www.prudential.com
Description: This is a national competition designed to reward students who have served their communities through leadership or outstanding initiative. Students must have completed a volunteer service activity in the past year. Winners are chosen on the basis of their descriptions of their individual contribution in a community service activity that has taken place, in part, over the past year.
How to Participate: Participants must fill out an application and submit it to a principal or head of an officially designated organization by the last weekday in October.
Cost: None
Categories/Content Areas: Community Service
Ages/Grade Levels: Grades 5–12
Status: National
Time Commitment: October 31 is the application deadline.
Resources Needed: Application and community service within twelve months of the application.
Awards/Benefits: Local honorees receive a certificate. State winners receive $1,000; an engraved silver medallion; and an all-expenses-paid trip to Washington, DC, for national recognition events. National honorees receive an additional $5,000, an engraved gold medallion, trophies for their school or organization, and a $5,000 grant to donate to the nonprofit organization of their choice.

Scholastic Art and Writing Awards

Contact: Alliance for Young Artists & Writers, Scholastic Art and Writing Awards, 557 Broadway, New York, NY 10012. Phone: 212-389-6100. Fax: 212-389-3939. E-mail: a&wgeneralinfo@scholastic.com.
Web Site: http://www.scholastic.com
Description: The Scholastic Art and Writing Awards recognize outstanding visual arts performance in fourteen categories and writing performance in eleven categories.

How to Participate: Individuals may submit an original entry accompanied by an entry form.
Cost: None
Categories/Content Areas: Composition/Language Arts
Ages/Grade Levels: Grades 6–12
Status: National
Time Commitment: The regional competition takes place throughout the school year; the national competition takes place in June and July.
Resources Needed: Scholastic Writing Awards entry form, or the portfolio entry form for the portfolio awards and scholarship nominations
Awards/Benefits: Regional awards include lapel pins and certificates, the Silver and Gold Key Awards, Honorable Mention Awards, and nominations for the American Visions and Voices Award. National awards include the Silver and Gold Awards, American Visions and Voices Awards, Silver and Gold Portfolio Awards, Teacher's Portfolio Awards, and Notable Achievement Awards.

Science Olympiad

Contact: Science Olympiad; 2 Trans Am Plaza Dr., Ste. 415; Oakbrook Terrace, IL 60181.
Web Site: http://www.soinc.org
Description: In the Science Olympiad, teams of fifteen students compete in tournaments held at local, state, and national levels. These interscholastic competitions consist of a series of thirty-two individual and team events that evaluate science concepts and knowledge; science processes and thinking skills; and science application and technology in biology, earth science, chemistry, physics, problem solving, and technology. Specific rules are available for each event.
How to Participate: A school team membership fee must accompany the completed membership application form thirty days before the regional or state tournament. This fee entitles the member school to a copy of the Science Olympiad *Coaches and Rules Manual* and entitles up to fifteen students to participate at the first level of competition in the district, regional, or state tournament.
Cost: The national fee is $55 for a fifteen-person team for Divisions B and C. The fee is $10 for Division A-1 and $15 for Division A-2. States/regions may add another, similar fee. Add 20% for shipping and handling for international membership. A set of fifteen student manuals for Divisions B and C can be purchased for $40; individual copies are $2.70 each for more than 15 or $5 each for fewer than 15.

The following videotapes are available for purchase:

Item	Cost
Elementary A 1 Fun Day	$30
Elementary A2 Video	$30
White House Video	$15
NSO* Finals (CO/89)	$30
NSO Finals (MO/91–33 min)	$40
NSO Finals (MO/91–9 min)	$30
NSO Finals (AL/92–30 min)	$45
NSO Finals (AL/92–10 min)	$35
BRIDGES from 1990 & 1991 National Finals	$30
NSO Finals-B (CO/93–32 min)	$45
NSO Finals-C (CO/93–40 min)	$45

*NSO = National Science Olympiad.

Categories/Content Areas: Biology, Earth Science, Chemistry, Physics, Technology/General Problem Solving
Ages/Grade Levels: Division A-1 (Grades K–3), Division A-2 (Grades 3–6), Division B (Grades 6–9), and Division C (Grades 9–12)
Status: State, regional, and national
Time Commitment: Variable
Resources Needed: One coach minimum, Science Olympiad membership form, coach's manual, and rules. Videotapes and student manuals may be purchased at an additional cost.
Awards/Benefits: Athletic-style medals are given for each event. In addition, championship trophies are awarded to the Division B and C school teams that compile the most total points during the Olympiad. The state receives a free set of first-, second-, and third-place medals and trophies. Fees for room and board so that state directors can attend a meeting that follows the national tournament are also paid.

Scripps Howard National Spelling Bee

Contact: Carolyn Andrews. Fax: 513-977-3803. Phone: 513-977-3040.
Web Site: http://www.spellingbee.com
Description: The National Spelling Bee encourages the improvement of spelling skills, the broadening of vocabulary, the acquisition of language concepts, and the development of grammatical skills.
How to Participate: Contests are held at the classroom and school levels and progress to the city, district, regional, state, and national levels.
Cost: None
Categories/Content Areas: Spelling/Language Arts

Ages/Grade Levels: Students less than 16 years of age; Grades 1–8
Status: National
Time Commitment: Competition at the various levels takes place throughout the school year.
Resources Needed: Contact the national office for details.
Awards/Benefits: Most sponsoring newspapers offer prizes to local finalists. Each national championship competitor receives a sightseeing trip to Washington, DC, and a chance to compete for prizes that total more than $30,000 in cash.

Sea World/Busch Gardens/Fujifilm Environmental Excellence Awards

Contact: Sea World/Busch Gardens/Fujifilm Environmental Excellence Awards, c/o Sea World Orlando Education Dept., 7007 Sea World Dr., Orlando, FL 32821.
Web Site: http://www.seaworld.org
Description: This awards program recognizes students and teachers who work to preserve the environment at the grassroots level. Applicants submit descriptions of projects they have developed that demonstrate significant environmental accomplishments.
How to Participate: Students complete the application form, which can be found online at the Web site listed above; ponder the criteria; and then form teams to type a fifteen-page maximum paper presentation. Materials are then submitted to the address listed above by the deadline.
Cost: None
Categories/Content Areas: Environment/Language Arts
Ages/Grade Levels: Grades K–12
Status: National
Time Commitment: All resources must be submitted by late November. Check the Web site for each year's specific deadline.
Resources Needed: Application form and paper presentation criteria, which can be found online. Students may also visit the Web site to see past winners and get ideas for their project topic.
Awards/Benefits: Eight winning groups each year win $10,000, an all-expenses-paid trip to an Anheuser-Busch theme park, a Fujifilm digital camera, one hundred T-shirts, and certificates. One environmental educator/leader each year receives $5,000.

Siemens Foundation Competition in Math, Science, and Technology

Contact: Siemens Foundation, 170 Wood Ave. S., Iselin, NJ 08830. Phone: 877-822-5233. E-mail: foundation.us@siemens.com.

Web Site: http://www.siemens-foundation.org

Description: This competition aims to reward students for excellence in math and science for research projects.

How to Participate: There are three phases to the competition. Students may enter as individuals or teams. Projects are reviewed by a panel of judges, and 300 projects are selected in October to compete in the regional competition in November, where students present a poster and make an oral presentation, followed by a question-and-answer session. Winners from each region compete in the national final in December in New York City.

Categories/Content Areas: Math/Science/Technology

Ages/Grade Levels: Secondary

Status: National

Time Commitment: Regional finalists are decided in October, regional competitions occur during November, and the national finals are in December.

Resources Needed: Students and/or teams must register online at the Web site listed above. Participants need skills in research and math, science, and/or technology. The Web site also provides participants with important competition information.

Awards/Benefits: The winners of each region receive a silver medal and scholarships of $3,000 (team members receive $6,000, to be divided equally among team members). These students also go on to compete at the national event in New York City. The runner-up teams win bronze medals and $1,000 scholarships. In addition, regional winners' names are also posted on the Siemens Foundation Web site.

The high school of the regional finalists receives a $2,000 award, to be used to support science, mathematics, and technology programs in that school. At the national level, the winning team or individual receives $100,000 in scholarships. Runners-up receive scholarships that range from $10,000 to $50,000.

Society of Professional Journalists High School Essay Contest

Contact: High School Essay Contest, Society of Professional Journalists, 3909 N. Meridian St., Indianapolis, IN 46208.

Web Site: http://www.spj.org

Description: This essay contest aims to increase students' knowledge and understanding of the importance of free media.

How to Participate: Participants must submit the entry form along with an essay of 300–500 words. Entries should be sent to the participant's local chapter. If the participant does not have a local chapter, then entries can be sent to the address listed above. Winners at the local chapter will be forwarded to the national competition.

Cost: None
Categories/Content Areas: Language Arts
Ages/Grade Levels: Secondary
Status: National
Time Commitment: Entries must be postmarked by March 1.
Resources Needed: Entry form and the signature of a sponsoring teacher. The Web site contains judging criteria, rules, and regulations.
Awards/Benefits: Winners receive scholarships: First place receives $1,000, second place receives $500, and third place receives $300.

Student Science Fiction and Fantasy Contest

Contact: Student Science Fiction and Fantasy Contest, P.O. Box 314, Annapolis Junction, MD 20701. E-mail: contest@bucconeer.worldcon .org.
Web Site: http://www.bucconeer.worldcon.org
Description: Sponsored by the L.A.con IV, the sixty-fourth World Science Fiction Convention, and Baltimore Worldcon, this competition evaluates short stories and artwork that have a science fiction or fantasy theme, as well as science essays.
How to Participate: Complete a contest entry form and send it, with a short story, piece of artwork, or essay, to the address listed above.
Cost: None
Categories/Content Areas: English/Language Arts
Ages/Grade Levels: Elementary age (Grade 5 and below), Middle school (Grades 6–8), High school (Grades 9–12)
Status: Local, regional, state
Time Commitment: Varies by participant
Resources Needed: None
Awards/Benefits: A participation certificate is given to each entrant. Finalists and semifinalists attend L.A.con IV; winners attend all five days of L.A.con IV.

Thespian Playworks

Contact: Thespian Playworks, 2343 Auburn Ave., Cincinnati, OH 45219-2815.
Web Site: http://www.edta.org
Description: This is a playwriting and script development workshop for students. Students submit manuscripts for review, and up to four will be selected for workshop readings and development at a thespian festival in Lincoln, Nebraska.
How to Participate: Participants must be active members of the Thespian Society who are enrolled in high school. Participants submit

entries beginning October 1 and postmarked no later than mid-February. Check the Web site listed above for the specific date for the year of interest. Plays must be original, with single authorship. Plays can be about any subject but may not be musicals or plays with copyrighted songs or lyrics. Send manuscripts to the address listed above.
Cost: Finalists must pay their own way to the thespian festival. Registration and room and board will be paid by the Thespian Society.
Categories/Content Areas: Language Arts
Ages/Grade Levels: Secondary
Status: National
Time Commitment: Play production time varies. Manuscripts must be submitted by mid-February. In addition, students must be available for a week in late June to attend the thespian festival.
Resources Needed: Two good, clean copies of the manuscript; a cover page; and a week of time in late June to attend the festival.
Awards/Benefits: Winners have an opportunity to develop their scripts with other actors and directors during the thespian festival. After a week of polishing, plays are read in staged readings for an audience.

ThinkQuest

Web Site: http://www.thinkquest.org
Description: This contest promotes interactive learning and technology. Students participate as teams to design innovative and educational Web sites.
How to Participate: Form a team and recruit a teacher to serve as the coach. The teacher enters the team in the competition by using a form that can be found on the Web site listed above. Teams then create Web sites on a topic of their choosing. A list of educational categories teams can choose from can be found on the Web site.
Cost: None
Categories/Content Areas: Computers/Language Arts/Technology/ also varies with Web site content
Ages/Grade Levels: Ages 9–19
Status: International
Time Commitment: Varies. The contest opens in August, and the entry deadline is in April.
Resources Needed: A teacher to act as a coach; Internet access; and team submission form, which can be found online. Teams may also want to visit the Web site to see past entries and more contest information.
Awards/Benefits: The top ten teams in each age group receive laptop computers and a cash award for the coach's school. The top three teams travel to ThinkQuest Live to celebrate their achievements. There is also a special award for the team that best demonstrates

global perspectives. Every team that submits a Web site has it published on the ThinkQuest library, an online resource.

Toshiba National Science Teachers Association/ExploraVision Awards Program

Web Site: http://www.exploravision.org
Description: This contest is designed to encourage students to use their knowledge, imagination, and science to create future technology. Students work in groups of two, three, or four with a teacher and optional mentor. Each team will select a technology that affects their lives and investigate what the technology does and how it works. Students will also question why, how, and when the technology was invented and then predict what the technology will look like in twenty years.
How to Participate: Teams must submit a report that includes a written description and graphics. The Web site listed above provides step-by-step instructions.
Cost: None
Categories/Content Areas: Science
Ages/Grade Levels: Grades K–12
Status: National
Time Commitment: Varies. Entries are due January 30.
Resources Needed: Computer, writing skills, some graphic skills
Awards/Benefits: National finalist teams and their mentors/guardians will be flown to Washington, DC, to be recognized at the ExploraVision Awards Weekend. The four members of the four first-place teams will receive a $10,000 U.S. Savings Bond. The four members of the four second-place teams will receive a $5,000 U.S. Savings Bond. Twenty-four teams will be regional winners, and they will receive a notebook computer for each winning school and a gift for each participant, including teachers and mentors. Each team member who enters will receive a certificate and small gift.

UNA–USA National High School Essay Contest

Contact: United Nations Association of the United States of America, 801 Second Ave., New York, NY 10017.
Web Site: http://www.unausa.org
Description: This essay contest was designed to inspire students to engage in global issues. The contest encourages students to come up with their own conclusions by thinking critically about issues they learn about in the classroom.

How to Participate: Students submit essays of 1,500 or fewer words. Students should contact their local United Nations Association chapter for entry information and each year's topic.
Cost: None
Categories/Content Areas: Language Arts/Social Studies
Ages/Grade Levels: Secondary
Status: National
Time Commitment: Winners are notified in mid-February.
Resources Needed: A local United Nations Association or chapter, access to the Web site listed above
Awards/Benefits: First prize wins $3,000 and a trip to New York City for the association's national convention. Second place receives $1,500, and third place receives $750.

USA Biology Olympiad

Contact: Center for Excellence in Education; 8201 Greensboro Dr., Ste. 215; McLean, VA 22102.
Web Site: http://www.cee.org
Description: This competition focuses on stimulating students' intellectual curiosity and developing their critical thinking skills in biological reasoning. It aims to encourage excellence in biology students.
How to Participate: The USA Biology Olympiad is a four-tiered competition. The first step is a multiple-choice examination administered nationwide to all interested students who have been nominated by their teachers. Then, the top 10% or top 500 examinations are eligible to take the USA Biology Olympiad (USABO) semifinal examination, a two-hour multiple-choice and short-answer test that also is administered at the school. The top twenty semifinalists are invited to attend the USABO Olympiad at a leading university. Interested students should inform their teachers, and teachers should register their school/class on the Web site.
Cost: There is no cost for students. Schools must pay a one-time registration fee of $75.
Categories/Content Areas: Science (Biology)
Ages/Grade Levels: Secondary
Status: National
Time Commitment: Teacher registration begins in early October. The open examination is administered in February. The national finalists have a two-week intensive training.
Resources Needed: Teachers must register their school online and pay the one-time registration fee. Teachers and students should visit the USABO Web site listed above for important information on rules and regulations, dates, helpful links, and materials to prepare for the examinations.

Awards/Benefits: All semifinalist participants, their teachers, and schools receive awards and recognition at local ceremonies. Finalists receive an all-expenses-paid trip to the USABO . The top four finishers at the national level are selected to represent the United States in the International Biology Olympiad.

U.S. Academic Decathlon

Contact: Mylene Chafe, Director of Operations/Customer Service and Accounts, U.S. Academic Decathlon, P.O. Box 1834, Council Bluffs, IA 51502-1834. Phone: 712-326-9589. Fax: 712-366-3701.
Web Site: http://www.usad.org
Description: The U.S. Academic Decathlon is a ten-event team competition. Each student competes in all ten events: (1) Art, (2) Economics, (3) Essay, (4) Interview, (5) Language and Literature, (6) Mathematics, (7) Music, (8) Science, (9) Social Science, and (10) Speech.
How to Participate: Enter a team of nine students: three Honor students (grade-point average [GPA] = 3.75–4.00), three Scholastic students (GPA = 3.00–3.74), and three Varsity students (GPA = 2.00–2.99).
Cost: For coaches and team members, the costs are as follows:

Product	Cost*
Basic Curriculum Package (set of 10)	$385.00
Curriculum Package Plus (set of 10)	$503.00
Individual Study Guides	$1.85

*Shipping cost is 10% of the order price or $3 for orders of $30 or less.

     Copyrighted individual materials may be ordered by schools only after the initial purchase of one or more of the Curriculum Packages. Additional materials available for purchase include Study and Resource Guides, Art Reproductions Booklet, Music CD, Practice Tests, Coaches Handbook, Flash Cards, and Scoring Software.
Categories/Content Areas: Super Quiz, a new theme each year; also Economics, Fine Arts/Language Arts, Mathematics, Science, Social Studies, Speech
Ages/Grade Levels: A team consists of nine full-time students from the ninth through twelfth grades of the same high school.
Status: Local, regional, state, and national. Currently, forty states participate.
Time Commitment:

May	Study guide released
June, July, August	Research and reading by large group
September	Practice test booklet released; teams formed

November	Local competitions
February	Regional competitions
March	State competitions
April	National finals

Resources Needed: Curriculum Package, practice tests, Super Quiz information, and possibly other study materials

Awards/Benefits: Gold, silver, and bronze medals are awarded in each category and each event. Overall individual winners are recognized, as are champion teams. Regional trophies were awarded for the first time in 1992. Each state's championship team advances to the national finals. There are also team awards in the Super Quiz and for overall ranking. There also is a small-schools division.

USA Computing Olympiad

Contact: USACO (USA Computing Olympiad); c/o Donald T. Piele; University of Wisconsin, Parkside; Kenosha, WI 53141-2000. Phone: 414-595-2231. Fax: 414-595-2056. E-mail: piele@.uwp.edu.

Web Site: http://oldweb.uwp.edu

Description: The USACO's goal is to select a team of four students to represent the United States in the International Olympiad in Informatics (IOI). The multilevel competition, with Gold, Silver, and Bronze competition levels, begins with online computer program writing competitions. The Level 1 competition is available for beginning programmers. Competitions at this level are held about every three weeks and offer less time-consuming challenges. On the basis of their performance in online contests held during the academic year, students who competed in the Gold, Silver, and Bronze competitions are invited to attend the USA Invitational Computing Olympiad, a week-long series of competitions. The final round is an intensive week-long program that ends in the selection of four team members to represent the United States at the IOI.

How to Participate: Complete the official registration form available at the Web site listed above.

Cost: None

Categories/Content Areas: Technology

Ages/Grade Levels: Secondary

Status: National

Time Commitment: Level 1—about every three weeks, there is a problem that requires less than an hour; the Gold, Silver, and Bronze Levels involve a three- to five-hour competition each month. The final round takes place over a one-week period.

Resources Needed: Newsletter and registration form

Awards/Benefits: Students who qualify for the final round receive an all-expenses-paid trip to the finals at the University of Wisconsin,

Parkside. The USACO pays travel expenses to the IOI for the four students selected to the U.S. team.

USA Mathematical Olympiad

Contact: American Mathematics Competitions, 1740 Vine St., University of Nebraska, Lincoln, NE 68588-0658. Phone: 800-527-3690. Fax: 402-472-6087. E-mail: amcinfo@amc.unl.edu.
Web Site: http://www.math.unl.edu
Description: The USA Mathematical Olympiad is a three and one-half hour, five-question, essay proof examination (i.e., one in which participants provide proofs in an essay format).
How to Participate: Eligibility to take this examination is based on a student's performance on the American Invitational Mathematics Exam.
Costs: None
Categories/Content Areas: Mathematics
Ages/Grade Levels: Secondary
Status: The United States and Canada are divided into eleven examination regions. The regions are listed in the teacher's manual, which is included with the examinations.
Time Commitment: The examination takes three and one-half hours and is in late April. Preparation time varies.
Resources Needed: An invitation to participate
Awards/Benefits: The eight top scorers on the USA Mathematical Olympiad and their parents are honored at elaborate ceremonies in Washington, DC. All expenses for these winners are paid. The students receive recognition and many awards.

USA Mathematical Talent Search

Contact: USAMTS (USA Mathematical Talent Search), P.O. Box 2090, Alpine, CA 91903-2090. Phone: 619-445-0112. E-mail: usamts@usamts.org.
Web Site: http://www.usamts.org
Description: This talent search is a free contest primarily sponsored by the National Security Agency. This competition gives students a month to work out solutions and submit required written justifications for each problem. Problems range in difficulty to challenge regular high school students and the best students in the nation. Students can use any materials to help, but the material must be their own. The USAMTS consists of four rounds of five problems that are posted and submitted online. Students accumulate points throughout the school year.

How to Participate: Students must complete entry and registration forms. Each round of problems is posted on the USAMTS Web site (listed above) at least four weeks before the solution is due. Students are asked to submit solutions to at least two problems in each round. Students earn five points for each correct, well-written answer and can earn up to one hundred points throughout the school year.

Cost: None

Categories/Content Areas: Mathematics/Technical Writing

Ages/Grade Levels: Middle and high school students

Status: National

Time Commitment: The rounds of competition span the school year. The time for solving problems varies according to the difficulty of the problem and the individual student.

Resources Needed: Internet access to register and receive/submit problems and solutions, registration form, and entry form

Awards/Benefits: Students develop problem-solving skills and improve their technical writing and math skills. The USAMTS is also one way students can enter the process of being selected for the USA Mathematical Olympiad team. In addition, the USAMTS score is necessary to qualify for the American Invitational Mathematics Examination, given by the American Mathematics Competitions. Students scoring in the following ranges are given certificates and book prizes:

Score	Prize
96–100	Gold Winner
76–95	Silver Winner
60–75	Bronze Winner
40–59	Honorable Mention

U.S. National Chemistry Olymplad

Contact: Cecilia Hernandez; USNCO (U.S. National Chemistry Olympiad) Coordinator; Room 834, 1155 16th St., NW; Washington, DC 20036. Phone: 800-227-5558, Extension 6169. E-mail: chernan dez@acs.org.

Web Site: http://www.chemistry.org

Description: The USNCO is the selection process for each year's U.S. representative to the International Chemistry Olympiad (IChO). High school students participate in the multitiered competition, which begins at the local level with written examinations, science fairs, or teacher recommendations. The top students from local competitions are invited to take the national examination, a three-part test that includes a multiple-choice section, a laboratory practical, and a free-response section. On the basis of the scores from the national examination, twenty students are invited to attend a two-week study camp at the U.S. Air Force Academy. At the camp, students study various topics in chemistry designated by the current year's IChO host country. Examinations and laboratory practicals determine the top four students from the camp, who are invited to participate in the IChO. At the IChO, the U.S. students compete in a five-hour laboratory practical and a five-hour theoretical examination.

How to Participate: Local sections of the American Chemical Society (ACS) and high schools work together to determine who participates. Contact the USNCO coordinator in Washington, DC, for details. Local sections use either the USNCO prepared examination, a local prepared examination, a laboratory practical, teacher recommendations, or regional events with competitive activities among teams to choose their nominees. Local sections of the ACS are vital to the success of the Olympiad program. The process begins in the fall, when local high schools are notified of the event. Local ACS sections use various means to nominate students to take the national examination. All students must be U.S. citizens who are enrolled in high school. To promote widespread participation, no more than two students from a given school may take the national examination.

Cost: None

Categories/Content Areas: Chemistry/General Problem Solving, Science

Ages/Grade Levels: High school

Status: National, international

Time Commitment: Local competitions/recommendations are done in March. The national examination is held in April. The Air Force study camp is two weeks in mid-June. The IChO is held in mid-July for one week. Opening ceremonies are on Monday; the laboratory examination is on Tuesday; and the written examination is on Thursday, with awards on Saturday.

Resources Needed: National examination

Awards/Benefits: Students have the opportunity to advance to an international competition. Gold medals are presented to students who score approximately in the top 10%, silver medals are awarded to the next 20%, and diplomas of recognition are given to the rest.

Vegetarian Resource Group Essay

Contact: Vegetarian Resource Group, P.O. Box 1463, Baltimore, MD 21203. Fax: 410-366-8804.

Web Site: http://www.vrg.org

Description: Entrants submit a two- to three-page essay on some topic related to being a vegetarian.

How to Participate: Submit an essay that has the entrant's name, address, telephone number, age, grade, school, and teacher's name to the address given above. Entrants do not have to be vegetarian.
Cost: None
Categories/Content Areas: Language Arts/English
Ages/Grade Levels: Three age divisions: Age 8 and under, Age 9–13, Age 14–18.
Status: National
Time Commitment: Entries must be postmarked by May 1; the time required to develop the essay varies by entrant.
Resources Needed: None
Awards/Benefits: A $50 U.S. Savings Bond is awarded in each age division.

Veterans of Foreign Wars Patriot's Pen

Contact: VFW (Veterans of Foreign Wars) Building, 406 W. 34th St., Kansas City, MO 64111. Phone: 816-756-3390, Extension 220. E-mail: swilson@vfw.org.
Web Site: http://www.vfw.org
Description: This essay contest is for sixth through eighth graders and was designed to give students an opportunity to write essays expressing their thoughts on democracy.
How to Participate: Participants submit an entry form and their essay to their local VFW post.
Cost: None
Categories/Content Areas: Language Arts
Ages/Grade Levels: Grades 6–8
Status: National
Time Commitment: The submission deadline is November 1.
Resources Needed: Entry form, which can be found on the Web site listed above; participants should visit the VFW Web site to locate a local post.
Awards/Benefits: Seventh- and eighth-grade students are eligible to receive U.S. Savings Bonds. The first-prize winner receives a $10,000 U.S. Savings Bond and an all-expenses-paid trip to Washington, DC.

Veterans of Foreign Wars Voice of Democracy Program

Contact: Gordon R. Thorson, Director, Youth Activities & Safety; 406 W. 34th St.; Kansas City, MO 64111. Phone: 816-756-3390.

Web Site: http://www.vfw.org

Description: The Voice of Democracy program, an audio essay competition, gives students the opportunity to voice their opinions about their responsibility to their country around a theme that is selected annually. The written essay cannot take less than three minutes or longer than five minutes to deliver. Quality of the audio, delivery, originality, and content are the basis for the judging.

How to Participate: Submit the entry form, the essay, and an audio recording of the essay to the local Veterans of Foreign Wars (VFW) post.

Cost: Price of the recording and postage

Categories/Content Areas: Government, Civics, History, Debate/Language Arts, Social Studies, Speech

Ages/Grade Levels: Grades 9–12 in a public, private, or parochial high school

Status: National, plus American schools overseas (dependents of U.S. military or U.S. civilian personnel can participate)

Time Commitment: Deadlines for completion of programs and judging are as follows:

School: mid-November

District: mid-December, but not before the week after the school/post program

Department: within first two weeks of January (by January 10)

Material to national headquarters: no later than mid-January (by January 15)

Resources Needed: Resource materials are available from the local VFW post.

Awards/Benefits: There are numerous opportunities to win scholarships and awards. Most VFW posts/auxiliaries offer monetary awards to program participants who place in their competition. The scholarship for the national student finalists who places first is $30,000, and the scholarship for the student finalist who places second is $16,000. Other finalists receive scholarships of lesser amounts. These scholarships are paid directly to the recipient's university, college, or appropriate school. All state winners receive an all-expenses-paid trip to Washington, DC.

VSA arts Playwright Discovery Program

Contact: *VSA arts* Playwright Discovery Program; 818 Connecticut Ave., NW, Ste. 600; Washington, DC 20006. Phone: 800-933-8721. Fax: 202-429-0868. E-mail: info@vsarts.org.

Web Site: http://www.vsarts.org
Description: Writers are invited to submit scripts that address issues regarding persons with disabilities. The theme, setting, and style are the author's choice. Scripts may be the work of a single author or multiple authors. Selected scripts are performed at the John F. Kennedy Center for the Performing Arts.
How to Participate: Along with an application and 250-word biographical description of the author or authors, submit three copies of a script for a one-act play that addresses some aspect of a disability. Previous Young Playwright Award recipients are not eligible. Students with and without disabilities are encouraged to participate.
Cost: None
Categories/Content Areas: Drama, Language Arts
Ages/Grade Levels: Ages 12–18, Grades 6–12
Status: National
Time Commitment: Script writing time varies by author.
Resources Needed: None
Awards/Benefits: Playwrights whose work is chosen, along with their chaperones, travel to Washington, DC, as guests of *VSA arts* to participate in rehearsals and to be honored at the premiere production of their play at the John F. Kennedy Center for the Performing Arts.

Weekly Mathematics Contest

Web Site: http://www.colstate.edu
Description: Weekly math problems are posted on the Web site listed above. The contest was designed to encourage enthusiasm and interest in mathematics. Answers are submitted online, and winners are chosen from the pool of correct answers.
How to Participate: Go to the Web site and click the link for "Problem of the Week." Solve the problem, and submit your answer online.
Cost: None
Categories/Content Areas: Mathematics
Ages/Grade Levels: The Elementary Brain Teaser is for students in Grades 6 and younger. Middle School Madness is for students in Grades 6–8. High School Challenge is for students in Grades 9–12.
Status: International
Time Commitment: Minimal
Resources Needed: Internet access
Awards/Benefits: Participants who submit correct solutions are listed online.

Weekly Reader's "What's Your Story?" Student Publishing Awards

Contact: Association of Educational Publishers; Attn: Weekly Reader "What's Your Story?" Student Publishing Awards; 510 Heron Dr., Ste. 309; Logan Township, NJ 08085. Phone: 856-241-7772. E-mail: mail@ aepweb.org.
Web Site: http://www.aepweb.org
Description: This contest is sponsored by *TIME* magazine and was designed to encourage students to strive for excellence in publishing. This program honors the best works of nonfiction and individual writing.
How to Participate: Participants submit three copies of their original work, accompanied by an entry form, to the address listed above, before the deadline (March 30).
Cost: $40 entry fee
Categories/Content Areas: Language Arts
Ages/Grade Levels: Grades K–12
Status: National
Time Commitment: The entry period is October 1–March 16. The late entry deadline is March 30.
Resources Needed: Entry form, which can be found online at the Web site listed above; three copies of the participant's entry; and the entry fee.
Awards/Benefits: Each winner receives a $500 check and will be invited to Washington, DC, in June, to be honored.

West Point Bridge Design Contest

Web Site: http://bridgecontest.usma.edu
Description: This contest is offered by the U.S. Military Academy. It is designed to introduce students ages 13 through Grade 12 to engineering. The task for participants is to design the least expensive bridge that will pass a simulated load test.
How to Participate: Visit the Web site listed above and download the Bridge Designer software. Then participants use the software to design a bridge, register their team, log in, and submit as many entries as desired.
Cost: None
Categories/Content Areas: Engineering/Technology
Ages/Grade Levels: Ages 13 through Grade 12. Anyone may enter the Open division.
Status: National
Time Commitment: Varies. The contest begins in January.
Resources Needed: Internet access and Bridge Designer software

Awards/Benefits: Varies with year, but all students have the opportunity to experience and learn the pleasures of engineering. The top ten teams in each zone receive a certificate.

WordMasters Challenge

Contact: WordMasters Challenge, 213 E. Allendale Ave., Allendale, NJ 07401. Phone: 201-327-4201. Fax: 201-327-6219.
Web Site: http://www.wordmasterschallenge.com
Description: Conducted at two levels—Elementary and Middle School Challenge and High School Challenge—and two divisions—Blue and Gold—at each level, this contest addresses vocabulary, verbal reasoning, word comprehension, and logical abilities. The Blue Division is for students of average to above-average reading and reasoning abilities, and the Gold Division is for students of superior abilities. A separate set of awards is issued to each division. The Elementary and Middle School Challenge concentrates on analogies based on relationships among words. The High School Challenge emphasizes reading comprehension. Each division has four competitions that are conducted at the participants' schools, and school personnel use contest answer keys to score responses. After each contest, the names and results of the ten highest scoring participants at each grade level are submitted to WordMasters on an official form that is provided along with other contest materials. The sum of these top ten scores is the team score.
How to Participate: Complete and return the registration form by the mid-October deadline. A school may enter grade-level teams in both divisions. Participating schools receive vocabulary lists.
Costs: Fees for elementary or middle school students are as follows:

One grade in either the Blue or the Gold Division: $80 for one year

One grade in both the Blue and the Gold Divisions: $130 for one year

Two different grades in either the Blue or the Gold Division: $160 for one year

Two different grades in both the Blue and the Gold Divisions: $260 for one year

Three different grades in either the Blue or the Gold Division: $240 for one year

Three different grades in both the Blue and the Gold Divisions: $390 for one year

The fee entitles each school to a grade-level series of three analogies meets (preceded by three vocabulary lists) and to a set of awards. A set of demonstration analogies can be ordered for an additional $7. For schools enrolling in both the Blue and Gold divisions, the fee is $80 per grade. In addition, districts enrolling five or more schools in the challenge are given an overall discount of 10%. Districts enrolling ten or more schools are given a discount of 20%.

Fees for high school students are as follows:

One grade: $95 for one year

Two grades in the same division: $170 for one year

Two grades in the same division and one grade in the other division: $265 for one year

All four grades: $340 for one year

Categories/Content Areas: Vocabulary, Verbal Reasoning/Language Arts

Ages/Grade Levels: Elementary and Middle School Challenge—Grades 3–8. The Blue Division is for students of average to above-average reading and reasoning abilities; the Gold Division is for students of superior abilities.

High School Challenge: Grades 9–12

Blue Division: Grades 9 and 10

Gold Division: Grades 11 and 12

The Blue Division is for students of average to above-average reading and reasoning abilities; the Gold Division is for students of superior abilities. A separate set of awards is issued to each division.

Status: National

Time Commitment: The Elementary and Middle School Challenge has three contests per year. The High School Challenge has four contests per year; each takes about thirty minutes. The amount of time spent preparing for each contest is up to the individual.

Resources Needed: Official enrollment form, vocabulary lists, demonstration analogies

Awards/Benefits: Each school receives medals and certificates to be awarded to the highest achieving students for the year.

Writer's Digest Annual Writing Contest

Contact: *Writer's Digest* Writing Competition, 4700 E. Galbraith Rd., Cincinnati, OH 45236.

Web Site: http://www.writersdigest.com

Description: For over 75 years, the *Writer's Digest* Annual Writing Contest has been rewarding writers for their work. Participants can write and compete in ten different categories.

How to Participate: The ten different categories are (1) Inspirational Writing (Spiritual/Religious), (2) Memoirs/Personal Essay, (3) Magazine Feature Article, (4) Genre Short Story (Mystery, Romance, etc.), (5) Mainstream/Literary Short Story, (6) Rhyming Poetry, (7) Non-Rhyming Poetry, (8) Stage Play (submitted by mail only), (9) Television/Movie Script (submitted by mail only), and (10) Children's/Young Adult Fiction. Participants can submit as many manuscripts as they wish. Competition rules, entry requirements, contest fees, deadlines, and judging criteria can all be found on the Web site listed above.

Cost: Poems are $10 for the first entry and $5 for each additional poetry entry submitted during the same online session. All other entries are $15 for the first entry and $10 for each entry submitted during the same online session. Entries postmarked after the deadline must pay an additional $2 per manuscript.

Categories/Content Areas: Language Arts/Journalism

Ages/Grade Levels: Participants must be at least 16 years old

Status: Not listed, although competition entries must be in English.

Time Commitment: The submission deadline is in mid-May. The specific date varies by year, and participants should check the Web site for this date.

Resources Needed: Entry fee and entry form found online. Play and script submissions must be mailed; all other entries may be submitted online.

Awards/Benefits: The Grand Prize winner receives $3,000 and a trip to New York City to meet with agents and editors. First-prize winners in each category receive $1,000, a manuscript critique and marketing advice, and $100 worth of *Writer's Digest* books. Second-place winners in each category receive $500 cash and $100 worth of *Writer's Digest* books. Third-place winners receive $250 cash as well as $100 in *Writer's Digest* books. Fourth-place winners receive $100 cash, fifth-place winners receive $50 cash, and sixth- through tenth-place winners each receive $25 cash. First- through tenth-place winners also receive a copy of the *2008 Writer's Market Deluxe Edition* and a one-year subscription (new or renewal) to *Writer's Digest* Magazine;

eleventh- through hundredth-place winners receive a certificate honoring their accomplishment.

Young Epidemiology Scholars Program

Contact: Young Epidemiology Scholars Program; 11911 Freedom Dr., Ste. 300; Reston, VA 20190. Phone: 800-626-9795, Extension 5932. E-mail: yes@collegboard.org.
Web Site: http://www.collegeboard.com
Description: This competition calls for research projects. These projects should use epidemiological methods of analysis to examine health-related issues. The contest seeks to encourage students to explore the environmental and social factors that affect health.
How to Participate: Participants must first create a collegboard.com user name and password. They then must complete a registration form and upload a research project. A mentor or advisor is optional.
Cost: None
Categories/Content Areas: Behavioral and Social Sciences/Physical Sciences
Ages/Grade Levels: High school juniors and seniors
Status: National
Time Commitment: The registration and submission deadline is February 1. The national event is held in April.
Resources Needed: Internet access; registration form, which can be found online at the Web site listed above; an optional mentor or advisor; and four days in April if you are a regional finalist
Awards/Benefits: Each year, up to 120 semifinalist students share as much as $456,000 in college scholarships. Two national winners will each receive a $50,000 scholarship. Regional finalists will be flown to Washington, DC, to compete with other finalists from their region. Twelve students will advance to the national finalist round.

Young Naturalist Awards

Contact: Young Naturalist Awards Administrator, American Museum of Natural History/NCSLET (National Center for Science Literacy, Education, and Technology), Central Park West and 79th St., New York, NY 10024-5192.
Web Site: http://www.amnh.org
Description: Entrants use the scientific method to conduct a research project in astronomy, biology, earth science, or ecology and then submit an essay in which they report their research and findings.

A scientific discovery or breakthrough is not required, but it is expected that the research will result in a new understanding. All work, including photographs, must be the original work of the entrant. Essay length varies by age division: Grades 7 and 8 write 500 to 2,000 words, Grades 9 and 10 write 750 to 2,500 words, and Grades 11 and 12 write 1,000 to 3,000 words. The maximum length of the final document, including all appendices, charts, drawings, photographs, and tables, may not exceed twenty pages. Criteria for judging essays include the investigative process and procedures followed, analysis and interpretation of data, documentation, interesting writing style, grammar and punctuation, and visuals.

How to Participate: Mail a completed application form and an essay that conforms to competition guidelines to the address given above.
Cost: None
Categories/Content Areas: English/Language Arts
Ages/Grade Levels: Grades 7–12
Status: National
Time Commitment: Varies by individual entrant
Resources Needed: None
Awards/Benefits: The best twelve essays are named as winners. These essays are posted on the museum's Web site, and the teacher of each winner receives a book collection. The twelve winners (two at each grade level) receive a scholarship as follows: seventh grade receives $500, eighth grade receives $750, ninth grade receives $1,000, tenth grade receives $1,500, eleventh grade receives $2,000, twelfth grade receives $2,500.

In addition, as many as thirty-six finalists receive $50 and a certificate of recognition, and as many as 300 semifinalists receive a non-cash award and a certificate of recognition.

Young Playwrights Festival

Contact: National Playwriting Competition; Young Playwrights, Inc., Dept. WEB; P.O. Box 5134; New York, NY 10185. Phone: 212-307-1140.
Web Site: http://www.youngplaywrights.org
Description: The Young Playwrights Festival provides a forum for review and evaluation of original scripts by a theater professional. Plays by individuals and groups of up to three writers are accepted; however, screenplays, musicals, and adaptations are not accepted.
How to Participate: Playwrights must be eighteen or younger on January 1. Mail a hard copy of the script to the address listed above by January 1. Electronic submissions will not be accepted, and scripts are not returned. All submissions must be by the author, not by a teacher or

parent. The scripts must be accompanied by a title page that lists the author(s) name, date of birth, home address, e-mail, and phone number.

Cost: None

Categories/Content Areas: Language Arts

Ages/Grade Levels: Age 18 or younger

Status: National

Time Commitment: Considerable time is involved in producing the play/script.

Resources Needed: Up-to-date registration information is available from the above address.

Awards/Benefits: Written evaluation of each play goes to the playwright; selected playwrights are invited to New York for a writers conference.

Web Sites for Finding Other Competitions

The following Web sites show lists of competitions that are periodically updated:

About: Mathematics
http://math.about.com

Department of Energy: Hydrogen, Fuel Cells, and Infrastructure Technology Program
http://www1.eere.energy.gov

Johns Hopkins University: Center for Talented Youth
http://cty.jhu.edu

K–12 Academic Competitions in the Yahoo? Directory
http://dir.yahoo.com

National Honor Society and National Junior Honor Society
http://www.nhs.us

National Science Teachers Association
http://www.nsta.org

Web World
http://www.webworldindex.com

Writers Digest
http://www.writersdigest.com

Index of Competitions by Title

FIRST Robotics Competition

First Step to Nobel Prize in Physics

First Young Adult Novel

Foundations for Life National
    Essay Program & Contest

Frazier Institute Student Essay Contest

Freedoms Foundation National Awards Program

Future City Competition

Future Problem Solving Program

George S. & Stella M. Knight Essay Contest

Harry Singer Foundation Essay Contests

Harvard–MIT Mathematics Tournament

High School Communications Competition

"Idea of America" Essay Contest

Intel International Science and Engineering Fair

Intel Science Talent Search

International Brain Bee

International Mathematics Olympiad

International Student Media Festival

Invent America!

Invitational Mathematics Examination

Jane Austen Society of North America Essay Contest

Japan Bowl

JFK Profiles in Courage Essay Contest

Joseph S. Rumbaugh Historical Oration Contest

Junior Engineering Technical Society Tests of Engineering Aptitude,
    Mathematics, and Science

Junior Science and Humanities Symposia

Kids Are Authors

KidsBookshelf Contests

Kids Can Write Contest

National Geography Bee

National German Test

National Greek Examination

National High School Oratorical Contest

National High School Student Solar Design Contest

National History Day

National Latin Exam

National Mythology Exam

National Peace Essay Contest

National Portuguese Exam

National Schools Project Poetry Contest

National Science Bowl

National Science Decathlon

National Science Olympiad

National Society of Black Engineers Try-Math-A-Lon Competition

National Spanish Exam

National Vocabulary Championship

National Women's Hall of Fame Essay and New Media Contest

National Young Astronomer Award

Nob Yoshigahara Puzzle Design Competition

Odyssey of the Mind

Ohio State University Press *The Journal* Award in Poetry

Olympiad of Spoken Russian

Panasonic Academic Challenge

Physics Bowl

President's Environmental Youth Awards

Program to Recognize Excellence in Student Literary Magazines

Promising Young Writers

Prudential Spirit of Community Awards

Scholastic Art and Writing Awards

Index of Competitions by Subject Area and Level

Elementary

Secondary

Alliance for Young Artists and Writers Scholastic Art and Writing Awards
All-USA High School Academic Team Competition
Amateur Poetry Contest
American Computer Science League
American Enterprise Speech Contest
American History Essay Contest
American Invitational Mathematics Exam
American Mathematics Competitions
American Regions Mathematics League
American Scholastics Mathematics Competition
American Society of Newspaper Editors, Quill and Scroll International Writing, Photo Contest
American Veterans (AMVETS) Americanism Program
Ann Arlys Bowler Poetry Contest
ARTS Recognition and Talent Search
Association of Educational Publishers Student Publishing Awards
Ayn Rand Essay Contest
Baker's Plays High School Playwriting Contest
BEST Robotics Competition
Biz Plan Competition
Botball Robotics
Canadian Open Mathematics Challenge
CANE Writing Contest
Christopher Columbus Awards
Civic Education Project: Civic Week
Clarke–Bradbury Science Fiction Competition
Classical Association of New England
Concord Review Emerson Prize
Continental Mathematics League
Creative Writing Essay Contest
Cricket League Contest
Destination Imagination
Discovery Channel Young Scientist Challenge
Doors to Diplomacy
DuPont Challenge Science Essay Awards Program
Duracell/NSTA Scholarship Competition
eCybermission
Edventures Robotics Contest
EngineerGirl Essay Contest
Federal Reserve Bank Fed Challenge
Federal Reserve Bank Student Essay Contest
Fire Fighting Robot Contest
First Middle-Grade Novel Contest
FIRST Robotics Competition
First Step to Nobel Prize in Physics
First Young Adult Novel

National Biblical Greek Exam

National Canon Envirothon

National Catholic Forensic League Grand National Speech and Debate Tournament

National Consumers League: LifeSmarts

National Council on Economic Education and Goldman Sachs Foundation Economics Challenge

National Engineering Design Challenge (Javits-Wagner-O'Day/Junior Engineering Technical Society)

National Federation of Press Women High School Communications Contest

National Forensic League National Tournament

National French Contest (*Le Grand Concours*)

National Geography Bee

National German Test

National Greek Examination

National High School Oratorical Contest

National High School Student Solar Design Contest

National History Day

National Latin Exam

National Mythology Exam

National Peace Essay Contest

National Portuguese Exam

National Schools Project Poetry Contest

National Science Bowl

National Science Decathlon

National Science Olympiad

National Society of Black Engineers Try-Math-A-Lon Competition

National Spanish Exam

National Vocabulary Championship

National Women's Hall of Fame Essay and New Media Contest

National Young Astronomer Award

Nob Yoshigahara Puzzle Design Competition

Odyssey of the Mind

Ohio State University Press *The Journal* Award in Poetry

Olympiad of Spoken Russian

Panasonic Academic Challenge

Physics Bowl

President's Environmental Youth Awards

Program to Recognize Excellence in Student Literary Magazines

Promising Young Writers

Prudential Spirit of Community Awards

Scholastic Art and Writing Awards

Science Olympiad

Scripps Howard National Spelling Bee

Sea World/Busch Gardens/Fujifilm Environmental Excellence Awards

Siemens Foundation Competition in Math, Science, and Technology
Society of Professional Journalists High School Essay Contest
Student Science Fiction and Fantasy Contest
Thespian Playworks
ThinkQuest
Toshiba National Science Teachers Association/ExploraVision
    Awards Program
UNA–USA National High School Essay Contest
USA Biology Olympiad
U.S. Academic Decathlon
USA Computing Olympiad
USA Mathematical Olympiad
USA Mathematical Talent Search
U.S. National Chemistry Olympiad
Vegetarian Resource Group Essay
Veterans of Foreign Wars Patriot's Pen
Veterans of Foreign Wars Voice of Democracy Program
VSA arts Playwright Discovery Program
Weekly Mathematics Contest
Weekly Reader's "What's Your Story?" Student Publishing Awards
West Point Bridge Design Contest
WordMasters Challenge
Writer's Digest Annual Writing Contest
Young Epidemiology Scholars Program
Young Naturalist Awards
Young Playwrights Festival

Foreign Language

AATSP Elementary/Middle School Poster Contest
Japan Bowl
National Biblical Greek Exam
National French Contest (*Le Grand Concours*)
National German Test
National Greek Examination
National Latin Exam
National Portuguese Exam
National Spanish Exam
Olympiad of Spoken Russian
Panasonic Academic Challenge

General Problem Solving

Academic Triathlon
Biz Plan Competition

Destination Imagination
Future Problem Solving Program
Invent America!
Let's Get Real
National Engineering Design Challenge (Javits-Wagner-O'Day/
    Junior Engineering Technical Society)
Nob Yoshigahara Puzzle Design Competition
Odyssey of the Mind
National Society of Black Engineers Try-Math-A-Lon Competition

Language Arts

Academic Games Leagues of America National Tournament
Academic Triathlon
Achievement Awards in Writing
Alliance for Young Artists and Writers Scholastic Art and Writing
    Awards
All-USA High School Academic Team Competition
Amateur Poetry Contest
American History Essay Contest
American Society of Newspaper Editors, Quill and Scroll International
    Writing, Photo Contest
American Veterans (AMVETS) Americanism Program
Ann Arlys Bowler Poetry Contest
ARTS Recognition and Talent Search
Association of Educational Publishers Student Publishing Awards
Ayn Rand Essay Contest
Baker's Plays High School Playwriting Contest
CANE Writing Contest
Clarke–Bradbury Science Fiction Competition
Classical Association of New England
Concord Review Emerson Prize
Creative Writing Essay Contest
Cricket League Contest
Destination Imagination
DuPont Challenge Science Essay Awards Program
EngineerGirl Essay Contest
Federal Reserve Bank Student Essay Contest
First Middle-Grade Novel Contest
First Young Adult Novel
Foundations for Life National Essay Program & Contest
Frazier Institute Student Essay Contest
Freedoms Foundation National Awards Program
George S. & Stella M. Knight Essay Contest
Harry Singer Foundation Essay Contests

Mathematics

Academic Games Leagues of America
    National Tournament
American Invitational Mathematics Exam
American Mathematics Competitions
American Mathematics Contest 8
American Regions Mathematics League
American Scholastics Mathematics Competition
Botball Robotics
Canadian Open Mathematics Challenge
Continental Mathematics League
eCybermission
Future City Competition
Harvard–MIT Mathematics Tournament
Intel Science Talent Search
International Mathematics Olympiad
International Student Media Festival
Invitational Mathematics Examination
Junior Engineering Technical Society Tests of Engineering Aptitude,
    Mathematics, and Science
Junior Science and Humanities Symposia
Knowledge Master Open
Mandelbrot Competition
MATHCOUNTS
Math Leagues
Math Olympiads for Elementary Schools
National Beta Club Convention
National Consumers League: LifeSmarts
National Engineering Design Challenge (Javits-Wagner-O'Day/
    Junior Engineering Technical Society)
National Science Bowl
National Society of Black Engineers Try-Math-A-Lon Competition
Panasonic Academic Challenge
Siemens Foundation Competition in Math, Science, and Technology
U.S. Academic Decathlon
USA Mathematical Olympiad
USA Mathematical Talent Search
Weekly Mathematics Contest

No School Involvement Required

Invent America!
League of American Poets Free Poetry Contest
National Biblical Greek Exam
National Consumers League: LifeSmarts

National Engineering Design Challenge (Javits-Wagner-O'Day/
   Junior Engineering Technical Society)
National High School Oratorical Contest
National Mythology Exam
National Vocabulary Championship
Nob Yoshigahara Puzzle Design Competition
Odyssey of the Mind
Ohio State University Press *The Journal* Award in Poetry
UNA–USA National High School Essay Contest
USA Mathematical Talent Search
Veterans of Foreign Wars Patriot Pen
Veterans of Foreign Wars Voice of Democracy Program
Weekly Mathematics Contest
West Point Bridge Design Contest
Young Epidemiology Scholars Program

Science

Botball Robotics
Christopher Columbus Awards
Clarke–Bradbury Science Fiction Competition
Destination Imagination
Discovery Channel Young Scientist Challenge
DuPont Challenge Science Essay Awards Program
Duracell/NSTA Scholarship Competition
eCybermission
Edventures Robotics Contest
EngineerGirl Essay Contest
Fire Fighting Robot Contest
FIRST Robotics Competition
First Step to Nobel Prize in Physics
Future City Competition
Intel International Science and Engineering Fair
Intel Science Talent Search
International Brain Bee
International Student Media Festival
Junior Engineering Technical Society Tests of Engineering Aptitude,
   Mathematics, and Science
Junior Science and Humanities Symposia
NAACP ACT-SO
NASA Space Settlement Contest
National American Indian Science and Engineering Fair
National Canon Envirothon
National Engineering Design Challenge (Javits-Wagner-O'Day/
   Junior Engineering Technical Society)
National High School Student Solar Design Contest

National Science Bowl
National Science Decathlon
National Science Olympiad
National Society of Black Engineers Try-Math-A-Lon Competition
National Young Astronomer Award
Panasonic Academic Challenge
Physics Bowl
President's Environmental Youth Awards
Science Olympiad
Sea World/Busch Gardens/Fujifilm Environmental
    Excellence Awards
Siemens Foundation Competition in Math, Science, and Technology
Toshiba National Science Teachers Association/ExploraVision
    Awards Program
USA Biology Olympiad
U.S. Academic Decathlon
U.S. National Chemistry Olympiad
West Point Bridge Design Contest
Young Epidemiology Scholars Program
Young Naturalist Awards

Social Studies

AAA High School Travel Challenge
Academic Games Leagues of America National Tournament
American History Essay Contest
American Veterans (AMVETS) Americanism Program
Civic Education Project: Civic Week
Concord Review Emerson Prize
Doors to Diplomacy
Federal Reserve Bank Fed Challenge
Federal Reserve Bank Student Essay Contest
International Student Media Festival
JFK Profiles in Courage Essay Contest
Joseph S. Rumbaugh Historical Oration Contest
Knowledge Master Open
National African American History Academic Challenge Bowl
National Beta Club Convention
National Council on Economic Education and Goldman Sachs
    Foundation
Economics Challenge
National Consumers League: LifeSmarts
National Geography Bee
National History Day
National Peace Essay Contest

Panasonic Academic Challenge
Prudential Spirit of Community Awards
UNA–USA National High School Essay Contest
Veterans of Foreign Wars Patriot's Pen
Veterans of Foreign Wars Voice of Democracy Program

Special Populations

NAACP ACT-SO
National Achievement Scholarship Program
National African American History Academic Challenge Bowl
National American Indian Science and Engineering Fair
National Society of Black Engineers Try-Math-A-Lon Competition
VSA arts Playwright Discovery Program

Speech

American Enterprise Speech Contest
Joseph S. Rumbaugh Historical Oration Contest
Modern Woodmen of America School Speech
National Beta Club Convention
National Catholic Forensic League Grand National Speech and
    Debate Tournament
National Federation of Press Women High School Communications
    Contest
National Forensic League National Tournament
National High School Oratorical Contest
U.S. Academic Decathlon
Veterans of Foreign Wars Voice of Democracy Program

Technology

American Computer Science League
BEST Robotics Competition
Botball Robotics
Continental Mathematics League
Destination Imagination
Fire Fighting Robot Contest
FIRST Robotics Competition
Intel International Science and Engineering Fair
NAACP ACT-SO
Panasonic Academic Challenge
ThinkQuest
Toshiba National Science Teachers Association/ExploraVision
    Awards Program
USA Computing Olympiad

Index